J U N K

Get rid of the junk in your life and
experience life as it was meant to be.

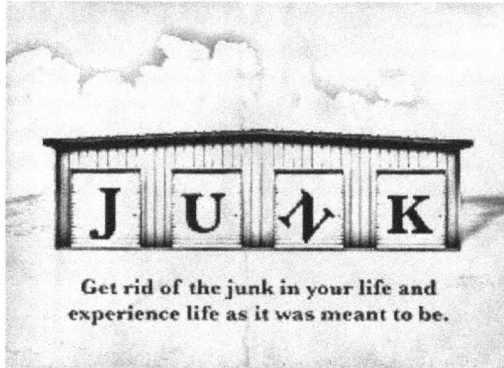

By Mitch Smith

Root Loud Publications
www.rootloudpublications.com

Cataloging-in-Publication Data is on file with the Library of Congress.

Unless otherwise indicated, all Scripture quotations are taken
from the Holy Bible, New International Version®. NIV®.
Copyright © 1973, 1978, 1984, by International Bible Society.
Used by permission of Zondervan. All rights reserved.
ISBN: 978-0-578-08146-5

CONTENTS

Foreword

Most self-help books focus on what readers don't have: self-confidence; body mass indexes of 24 or less; happy marriages; protected wealth; ideal jobs; well-adjusted children; youthful appearances; certain desired or marketable skills; and so on. Mitch Smith's book *Junk* strikes a louder and clearer chord, I think, because it so wryly and correctly asserts that what really limits and imprisons us is not what we DON'T have but what we DO have. Our possessions – and what we put into our heads and mouths – the author notices, actually possess us. They rob us of precious time, creativity, love, a sense of well being and freedom. What we so rabidly and rapidly consume, the author wisely sees, is really consuming us. We Americans are at a crossroads, Smith says, and it's time we take the road less traveled – the road where need trumps greed, quality beats out quantity, and less truly means more. I bet we'd all like to travel down that road. I know I would. It's the road where real living is there for the taking and the words if, but, only and when aren't necessary. And step by step, in his book, the author explains how to start that trek and keep going in the direction of having the good instead of having the goods.

Smith's story gets at the raw truth because it springs from it. Like many books that make a difference, *Junk* was conceived from a real human crisis. Doctors discovered that at age thirty-nine, Smith had a tumor, and with three companies to oversee, more board positions than he could count, an upcoming run for the state senate, and a third child on the way, he had to figure out a way to pare down his activities and decide what really mattered and what he could let go of. Along the journey to health, he also became aware and was astounded by the fact that the self-storage business was so utterly successful in this country – much more so than any other place in the world.

Simplifying and just cutting back do not begin to describe what Smith professes in *Junk*. What he gives us is so much more – his gift is the gift of a new world, it's a vision of what true living is, and it offers the potential to exist unencumbered by things, to enjoy a life we can afford and one where we have more time to spend with the people and pursuits we love. He promotes completely changing our habits, and he does so in a straightforward, but also humorous way. What Smith extends is strong medicine, but it actually goes down pretty easily.

Junk is anything but, and it's one thing, as you take on the great task of ridding your life of clutter, confusion, addictions and accumulations, you will want to purchase and possess. You know, I could go on and on about Mitch Smith and his book, but I know ('cause I've read it) when enough's enough. So there you go. Read it, heed it, and keep it close by.

Simon T. Bailey, is a Brillionaire and author of *Release Your Brilliance*. www.simontbailey.com

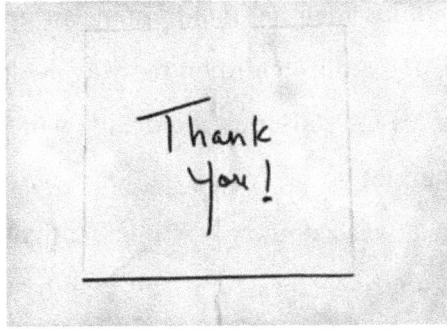

Acknowledgements

I have always found it interesting to read book and music acknowledgements. The order in which these acknowledgements place people has always made me wonder; is that the order of importance? I don't know exactly where to start, so I'll start with the really important people first and then move on down. How is that?

Thank you Jesus for coming down and showing us how to live a life without junk and making the sacrifice for my sins. (When Paul says he was the "chief of sinners," it evidently had not been revealed to him that I would be coming along 1950 years later.)

Thank you to my wife, Ashley, who has found some way to put up with me the last sixteen years. She is my best friend in life. I cannot imagine life without her. Her support in four business ventures and this book prove how patient she is and how much she must love me.

Thank you Erin, Boyd, and Mary Claire for making me laugh

everyday. Whether it is chasing you around the house being the "Tickle Monster," or sitting by campfires roasting marshmallows, I simply love having you in my life. The testimony in this book is for you and your children. I pray that I can live the rest of my life as a lasting legacy for you.

My Mom and Dad really did chose me. Thank you for adopting me at the age of five weeks and giving me a home full of love and encouragement. You taught me how to live with contentment and with love for one another. The testimony in this book is due to the testimony you laid before me.

Thank you Stone Crider for being my guardrail and hedge for fourteen years as an accountability partner. To Marion Davis, Joe Taber, Mike Blackwell, Ransey Bowers, and Edwin Davis who have invested countless hours in me. They have discipled me, taught me, and encouraged me everyday. They and their wives prayed for me and my family daily. Thank you.

For Will Haynie and Rick Mosteller, thank you for being a great example for me in college and re-directing my path to see life has purpose. When I didn't have the right direction and needed correction, you were there. I'd like to offer an eternal thanks to Buster Brown, Pastor of East Cooper Baptist Church, thank you for enabling me to encounter Jesus through amazing preaching. You taught me truth, and opened my eyes, ears, and heart to the Word. Thank you.

Thank you to Deena Bouknight and Jana Daley for not only editing my writing, but teaching a forty-three year-old how to write. Thank you to the more than one hundred employees I have had the blessing of working with through the years. I hope that I was (as I promised) "a mere stepping stone in your life to a higher place." And thank you to the countless people in my life who encourage me and love me for who I am. Thank you for showing me how to live life as it was meant to be.

Mitch

To my children, Erin, Boyd, and Mary Claire-
Thank you for putting a smile on my face everyday.

To my beautiful wife, Ashley- It is because of you that
I can boast of being the greatest salesperson in history.

Chapter 1

A Stop Sign and a Self-storage Unit

I have come to realize that junk in our lives is a giant problem. It was kind of like those old V8 commercials when the actor would bop himself on the head and say, "Wow, I could have had a V8!" Perhaps we all need to bop ourselves in the head and exclaim, "Wow! I could live much more simply."

That is kind of what happened to me with regard to my view of junk. Let me clarify up front; I am not a packrat. My personal rule is that if you have not used it in six months, you give it away, throw it away, or sell it. Here is the story of how I came to finally see junk in my life and in the life of others. I also came to see the ultimate cost it bears.

Visualize a long drive through a rural part of South Carolina. There are beautiful fields, plentiful cow pastures, and typical ranch houses sitting uncharacteristically beside double wide mobile homes. That morning's drive was taking me to see a wonderful, old friend. The trip's purpose was to spend some time with his wife and him prior to a major surgery he was about to have down in Charleston. I felt it was best for me to head down and visit with them, encourage him, and pray with both of them. I wanted to remind him that he needed to heal in less than eight weeks in order to make our annual fall mountain trip.

On my drive into this small town of two thousand residents, I came to a stop sign and noticed an odd sight. In this small town sat a self-storage facility that covered a large piece of real estate.

Who, out here, would have a need to rent a storage unit?

In this part of the world, if you have more stuff than your house can hold, you build a barn, a shed, or even a lean-to. Thanks to the invention of those blue plastic tarps, you even see lawn mowers, Rotor-tillers, and even cars rotting underneath these canopies. In such regions as this, double wide mobile homes are the residences of choice and many are sitting alongside a car on blocks, a bass boat, and a pickup truck.

A self-storage unit was about the last thing I would have expected to see in this remote area. I remember sitting at the stop sign for a couple of minutes asking myself, "How much stuff do people have that they would pay someone $50-plus a month to store, when they all probably have plenty of storage on their own property." I turned toward my friend's home and drove on thinking that what I had just witnessed made no sense, at least to me.

He and his wife lived in one of those small towns that used to thrive with local five-and-dime stores, meat and three restaurants, and pharmacies where you would get your favorite ice cream or malt. I sometimes reminisce about those small town days. Life was simple and you knew everyone by their first name. It was like Mayberry in the Andy Griffith Show.

As I pulled into his driveway, I was still chuckling at the thought of a self-storage unit on the outskirts of this town. When I walked in to greet my friend and his beautiful wife, we sat for about an hour discussing his upcoming surgery, the marriage of their daughter, and our upcoming men's retreat to the mountains. It was the normal discussion about family, work, and health.

As I checked the time, however, I realized that I needed to be heading back home for a business meeting. Yet, before I left, I couldn't resist asking my friend about the self-storage unit I had seen. As it turned out, he and his wife built it ten years ago to provide income for their retirement years. It had been a good investment with a good return.

You see, he was in construction and decided, through some investigation, that these units brought in a hearty income, especially into one's retirement years. Imagine having one hundred or more units paying you $50-plus a month per unit; that is more than $5,000 in monthly income. I found this to be remarkably smart as an investment, but downright crazy for the people paying for it out there in the country.

As I began asking questions, it became clear that this had been a successful venture, with minor headaches we'll discuss later. When I inquired about what these people were storing, he replied and chuckled, "You'd be amazed at the stuff they store." He mentioned that there was a motorcycle, a lot of old furniture, old appliances, old magazines, and the list goes on. He added, "To them it has value, but we'd just see it as junk."

My friend is a man of few words. When I asked him if there

was anything significant within the walls of his storage units, he replied, "Not much." He told me that since the day he built it, the units had, for the most part, stayed fully occupied. The other question that ran through my mind was this: If something did have value, wouldn't you want it close to you? Wouldn't you want to be able to put your hands on it? Wouldn't you want to see it to be sure it was okay? I guessed it wasn't as important in their lives as they thought it was.

As I left my friend and his wife, the thought of self-storage units was on my mind – even though, a few hours earlier, I had never given them a thought. I had never rented one and often thought they probably sat vacant. Once I started thinking about self-storage units, I then began to see how many there were within five miles of my home in Columbia, South Carolina. Self-storage units appeared to be on every major street around me.

I became increasingly aware of the amount of junk we acquire and pile into our lives. We buy so many things, mount the new items on top of old items in the closet, that all of it becomes totally useless to us. However, in some areas of our lives, we can take that excess junk and use it to benefit those in need around us. But instead of thinking of others, we think only of ourselves. We think that we may just wear that extra pair of shoes again, even though we have two other pairs just like them.

Consequently, the question that began dominating my mind

was: What junk do I have in my life that I need to get rid of? What keeps me from moving freely through my home, my work, and my life? Why do I hold on to things in my life that have lost their value, or their value continues to diminish? Why would I allow these things to hinder my ability to move, to live, and to grow?

My goal is for us to go through this journey together and rid our lives of junk that we don't need. Let's endeavor to move through life with freedom, and less burden. I want to experience a life free from junk. How about you?

Some questions to ask yourself

Are you currently using a self-storage unit? If yes, is the value of the items stored equal to (or less than) the total amount you'll pay for the storage unit in a twelve-month period? Example: The typical price for a storage unit for twelve months is $840 ($70/month). Is the value of the items in your unit worth $840 or less? tIf yes, what should you do?

If you don't use a self-storage unit, what junk in your life is taking up room that would be good to get rid of? It may reside in your attic or crawl space. It may be around your waist, between your ears, or in your heart.

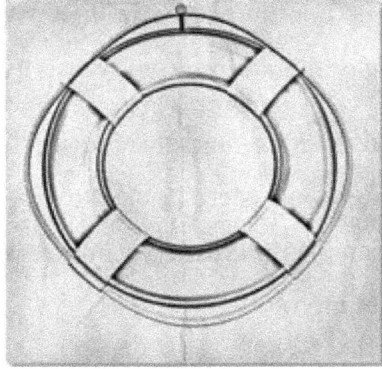

Chapter 2

Somebody Throw Me a Life Ring

Before we get too deep into this junk, let's review Merriam Webster's definition of "junk."

The definition we normally focus on is: "secondhand, worn, or discarded articles; clutter."

Another definition, which is the one we will use to help us in looking at junk, is: "something of little meaning, worth, or significance."

The word "significance" stands out clearly. What is significant? We would agree that people, places, or things that have the most value in our lives are significant. You don't want to live without them. They bring meaning to who you are. Here is an account of my personal junk, or the things of insignificance to which had attributed significant value:

Like driving in the country, coming to a stop sign in the middle of nowhere and getting a glimpse of something that was out-of-place, I came to a personal stop sign at the age of thirty-nine. In May of 2006, I was amazed to see the way I had filled my life to the max with commitments and activities. Life was overwhelming with daily calendars was jammed with activities from morning to early evening. There was constant travel, after-work non-profit board meetings, church duties, and after-work ballgames. Many of these activities were important to me. I cared about each one and tried to give them all my very best.

About that time, I began experiencing physical symptoms that I had never experienced before. On the advice of my insurance company, I first journeyed to my primary care physician with my symptoms. He made his diagnosis; however, he decided there could be more to it. Before I left the doctor's office, his team had scheduled an appointment for me with a specialist the following week. My cousin who happened to work for my doctor assured me that everything would be all right.

According to my doctor, nothing was urgent at the time, and I wasn't in pain. I did have some minor discomfort though, and it was the kind you don't want to live with too long. When I visited the specialist and described my symptoms to him, he began asking the 100 questions that all doctors feel obliged to ask. However, when he got to the questions on family history, we had to skip that section.

Because I was adopted when I was only five weeks old, I had no idea of my family history. As far as I am concerned, my adopted parents are my only parents. It has never crossed my mind to wonder who brought me into the world. This event didn't even trigger the desire to hire an investigator to find my birth parents and learn their medical history for my own sake. I am not a person who lives in yesterday. The past is merely that, and we cannot change it - only learn from it.

After the initial exam and some tests, the specialist recommended a colonoscopy. While he felt sure he knew what the issue was, a colonoscopy would clearly reveal any additional problems. With no family history, it was imperative to get to the root of this problem and determine what was really going on. Regretfully, I would have to wait an entire week before a colonoscopy could be scheduled.

Colonoscopies are not the easiest test I have ever encountered. All I remember before the procedure is talking to a nurse. The next thing I remember is slowly waking up to see a fuzzy, balding man standing over me. I immediately recognized him as my doctor. I didn't like the first thing he told me, however. "We found something," were the first words out of his mouth. I immediately replied back, "Those weren't quite the words I wanted to hear you say when we met again." I was still woozy from the anesthetic, it took me an hour before I could think about what the doctor had just said and coherently speak with him and my wife about the results.

The colonoscopy revealed a small mass, larger than a marble, at the end of my colon and adjacent to my appendix. The good news was the doctor was able to get a biopsy during the colonoscopy. The part I didn't like was that it would take five days to get the results. The colonoscopy was on a Thursday, and it would be Tuesday before I could find out what I might be in for. Being the most impatient person in the world, I exclaimed that there had to be a way to get results back quicker than five days. Diagnostic testing would reveal whether the tumor was malignant or benign.

Once we knew that, we could discuss next steps.

Before we get to Tuesday's news, let me tell you where I was personally in my life at that time. I had been fortunate, by this time, to be married to Ashley for ten great years. We had been blessed with our oldest daughter in 1999, a son in 2002 and another daughter in 2005. We lived in a home we had purchased, added onto, and remodeled exactly the way we wanted it. It was minutes from downtown, convenient to work and church, and located on a beautiful ten-acre lake. All was good and everything seemed to be as it should be. Or was it?

In business, I had many ups and a few downs. I started my first business in 1994 and saw it grow to become one of the leading companies in our industry. I sold the business in 1999, during the height of the dot-com era, to a group in Florida. This was a big mistake. I had no idea I had sold the company to the wrong people. When my wife met them for the first time six months after selling, she turned to me in the middle of the party and said; "Don't tell me we sold our company to these guys?" Women have this innate ability to see things that men just can't see. Her "woman's intuition" was absolutely correct.

Within months, we saw our eight years of work become nothing. "Oh", you say, "but you sold the company." Well, here was one of my biggest mistakes in life. Throughout our marriage, Ashley and I had been smart about our money. Even though she had previously worked as a pharmacist making great money, we lived off my income. We had agreed that when she became pregnant that she would stay at home. Having some money saved up and making a good income, I didn't need the immediate cash from the sale of the business and felt that taking stock instead could yield a good return. Regretfully, the stock I would take in this publicly held company would become worthless within two years. We would basically lose all of the investment.

A little more than a year after the sale of the company, I resigned. I took two weeks off with my wife and daughter and drove to Kiawah Island to write a business plan for my next company. When we returned, I met with two of my mentors, who would become the first two investors in my next venture. Within a matter of two weeks, we raised the money needed to launch the next company.

Having a godly man mentor me during those difficult years was one of the greatest experiences in my life. Marion Davis would invite me into his life and help me through mine. He is one of the finest men God has ever put in my life to encourage me and to walk with me. Sixteen years later, we still talk almost weekly. Our investment team included Marion's brother Edwin, Mike Blackwell, and Ransey Bowers. These men would gave me guidance in life, marriage, raising children, and business for the next eight years.

When my non-compete clauses expired for the first company

I sold, I started a similar company to provide software support services to large organizations in our new software venture. At that moment, I had a wife, three children, two companies, was organizing a third company, and was on more non-profit boards that I ever needed to be. In addition, I was serving at church as a deacon. At the time of my colon scare, I had so much on my plate. I was my own personal self-storage unit.

So with all this, you'd think I was through, right? Nope! I had announced three months prior to the tumor being found that I was running for state senate. And I was not running for any senate seat, I was running as a Republican against a twenty-six year Democratic incumbent.

I had a tremendously full life with no room to spare. I needed a personal self-storage unit for my life's junk at this point. Now, with my doctor adding yet another burden to carry, I knew I had some important decisions to make. It was at this point that I began to carefully look at the "stuff" in my life. I had to determine what was really significant to me and what wasn't.

What I really needed was to clean out the junk in my life. If my tumor was malignant, I would probably have to endure chemotherapy and treatment for colon cancer. If it was benign, I would have surgery and most likely no further treatment would be required. It was Thursday, and I was riding home from the hospital with my wife. You can imagine all of the things running through my head.

I did something on that Friday I never do. I called the office to let them know I would not be there for a few days. I am not a workaholic, but I certainly love what I do. I am so fortunate to wake up everyday desiring to do more.

It was time to think, prioritize, and pray this through. Thankfully, a pastor, Conrad "Buster" Brown, a mentor, Will Haynie, and a teacher, Rick Mosteller, showed me how to do this my senior year of college. Now ten years later, I would now lean on their teaching to help me prioritize my life.

Some questions to ask yourself

What items of "insignificance" are holding you back?

What insignificant items are occupying the space in your life that should have items of significance in that place?

Are Monday night football games robbing you of quality time with your wife and children?

Is going out with the girls more important than a date night with your husband?

Do you think it matters, at the end of your life, that you served on non-profit boards or spent hours in church committee meetings discussing trivial issues?

Chapter 3

The Bucket List

I think you will find that while these two stories are different, both give insight to the junk that is in our lives. One is basically a parable of the other. As I began to identify all of the physical, insignificant items that we keep around us, it was like a dejà vu moment. I had seen this before, just in a different light. After days of reflection on the self-storage units and identifying those useless items in my home, it occurred to me that I had actually been through this process before.

We don't intend to obsessively begin buying things just because the box is marked with the words "collector's series." We don't intend to walk into the mall and pull out our plastic to buy overpriced jeans just because they were worn by a gorgeous model on television. Our society is bombarded with marketing and advertising in every medium we encounter. The internet, radio, television, magazines, and billboards are intent upon getting you to do something you may not otherwise do. Being in the media business for over sixteen years, I know this to be a fact.

However, we need mental triggers in our life to correct our course and change our behaviors when we go astray. We need people we can trust around us who can be honest and ask the question, "Do you need that?" We need events that bring us back to reality. It may be taking a mission trip, working at the soup kitchen, or visiting a widow in the nursing home. Camping often provides the needed time of reflection for me, but ultimately, you have to find what helps you make those necessary adjustments in your life. I know the need for accountability. Why? Because I am just like you and have been shaped by the effects of my environment. If I don't have these people or things to remind me of what is a priority in my life, then you can guess what I'll resort to doing. I resort to what is best for me at the moment with no consideration of tomorrow.

I came across a verse recently that gives us insight to our hearts. In Jeremiah it says, "The heart is deceitful above all things." We all wish this wasn't the case, but if we reflect on our intentions and habits, we see dishonesty in many areas of our life. We even deceive ourselves when we tell ourselves we need to buy something we don't need. The verse ends with, "Who can understand it?" We can't. We will always scratch out heads and ask ourselves, "Why did I do that?" As I drove my last (note last) new car off the car dealership property, I thought to myself of how much value this car would lose as soon as I pulled onto the street. Ouch!

In the movie, *The Bucket List*, with Morgan Freeman and Jack Nicholson, both men are terminally ill. They meet at a cancer ward and through conversation about the things they wished they'd done, decide to leave, and start a road trip in order to accomplish a wish list of activities before they die. Not only is the movie funny, it is real. We all have dreams and desires we wish to accomplish in life. However, the bucket list at the end of our lives is about living;

and, the list at the beginning of our work life is about getting. In the movie, Freeman is a blue-collar mechanic and Nicholson is a very rich owner of many hospitals. In the movie, the economic circumstances of Freeman prohibit him from experiencing those things in life he has most desired. This is quite understandable. However, for Nicholson, his busy lifestyle prevented him from living those experiences his life yearned for. The clutter of his daily life kept him from living.

Because we are infected with junk in so many areas of our lives, this infection spreads to our churches, businesses, and non-profits. Therefore, we need to look within each one of these organizations and begin ridding them of their junk as well. Each of these are so bent on serving their own needs; they fail to serve the real needs around them. Whether it is the homeless, children, employees, or congregation members, their purpose in life is hidden for the junk that lives within each one of them. I cover these areas in more detail on the website www.getridofthatjunk.com.

Some questions to ask yourself

Have you ever created a bucket list of things you'd like to do before you die? If not, why not create that list today and love living?

In life, are you serving your needs or the needs of others? What does society tell us is more important? Which one does the Bible tell us?

Chapter 4

Junk Everywhere

We see junk everywhere. Especially when we travel around the good olé' Unites States of America, we're confronted with an abundance of stuff we have acquired that becomes junk. This doesn't include trash left mindlessly on our back roads and inter- states. This includes items of prior significance dissolving away to become nothing, yet still occupying space in our homes and lives.

Driving to the library last week to return yet another late book, I noticed a small, valuable piece of real estate with a rusting chain link fence beside the library. With grass up to your hips, six old cars sat rusting away. My question is: Who would allow a valuable piece of real estate to just sit there and become an eyesore? How much could it cost to merely remove these junk cars, cut the grass, and take down the fence? What a beautiful parcel of land it could be, even if nothing were on it but green grass- a compliment to the library instead of an unsightly blemish.

Junk, sometimes called "extra stuff sitting around," is plainly and simply junk. Whether it is in our homes, in our neighbor's garage, or our parent's attic, there are those things the simply need to go. They merely need to be removed and discarded in a manner that doesn't continue to occupy space within our lives any longer. The value has vanished. The usefulness has ceased. The need has been replaced. (Note: This does not include children, spouses or in-laws.)

Remember the old saying that "one man's junk is another man's treasure." My dad is one of those who will pick up someone else's junk beside the road. It sits there waiting for the next trash run. What is unique about my dad is that not only does he take it; he repairs it to amazing shape. If he can find a piece of furniture or a useful piece of something, he will take it, fix it, and then donate it to families in need. It is amazing what he can do with what is thrown away. His specialty is push lawn mowers. He might find three or four a year, completely repairing them and then giving them away. What a gift, and what a ministry. A positive outcome of junk!

The difference between junk and treasure is best seen in one of the Public Broadcasting Station's most followed shows, *The Antique Roadshow*, which is the garage sale version of Sotheby's, the most known and expensive auction house. While they don't auction the items on the show, the experienced antique dealers visit with hundreds and thousands of people in order to determine if that "rare find" in the attic or neighborhood yard sale yielded a treasure. In case you haven't watched the show, literally hundreds of people attend this traveling show. Experts walk through the crowd eyeing the items brought to see which will be featured on the show. People come from everywhere with everything imaginable. Some will carry the small piece in their hands, while others use furniture dollies to roll in their great-great grandmother's chest of drawers.

A good friend in the auction and estate business tells me that estate items will many times fail to get the value the family thinks they are worth. Remember, the buyer must attribute the same significance to that item in order to pay the buyer the price asked. The estate sales, where the family has held furniture and other items for many generations, are often letdowns for the children. The thought of the big return just isn't there.

I know we put value on things that have no real material value. We call it sentimental value. Usually those sentimental items are stored carefully and packed away neatly so that they'll last forever. Granted they may make it through a few generations, but if you think about it, what really happened to grandma's handmade quilt? What happened to great grandpa's pocket watch? Where is that broach that was worn by great-great-great grandmother during the Civil War?

We have these "items of sentimental value" in our family as well. For my wife, it is her grandmother's fine china. It still sits in the attic in the same box with the same tape put on it when we pushed it up there thirteen years ago when moving into our home. For me, it is my college uniforms and shako hat worn at the military college I attended twenty years ago. For my daughter, it is the Goofy hat from her first visit to Disney World. As you see, we all have sentimental items around us. The question is: How much space does it take up in your life and what value does it carry?

The times it hits home are when you try to find that particular item to show to a friend and you have so many items around that you can't see it sitting before you. The issue is clutter. You look on your walls and see shelves of old magazines you can't get rid of, nails holding tools you've used only once, and strings holding everything else. Everywhere you look, you see things. It is called clutter. You can have so much stuff in your garage, under the house, and in the attic that you really don't know what you have.

We collect so many things in life that we loose perspective on the real issue it causes. We become numb to this stuff. We start with nothing, make more money year by year, and acquire more and more. We store up and accumulate until we wake up years later, and we can't even walk through our own homes.

The gradual piling up of stuff, over time, becomes part of our normal lives. It is the proverbial frog in the boiling water. When you put the frog in cold water and turn on the heat, he'll just stay there to eventually die. If you tried to drop him into boiling water, he'll attempt to jump right back out. You don't just pile the junk into your home or life overnight. You begin attributing certain values to items in your possession.

If you have ever listened to the Dave Ramsey Show, you'll continually learn of people who have spending problems. Their spending is attributed to trying to look successful. They merely buy, trade, and buy again so that they can keep up with their neighbors (who are merely doing the same thing). Our society is compelled to live a lifestyle beyond their financial limits. They just can't stop spending money and can't resist applying for credit at every store. Dave is one of the best and most humorous teachers on modifying these behaviors I have ever seen. As Dave says, "Success is a pile of failure that you are standing on." His goal is to help you reach financial peace and freedom. He does not help you attain your income potential, but offers advice on simply modifying your spending potential, coupled with some guardrails to protect for those unexpected needs. As he points out, all this is 20% information and 80% behavior. Most people know what they should do, but they just don't have the behavioral discipline to carry it out. We don't need more information. We simply need application.

Dave and I recently became acquainted through a ministry on giving. It was here that he shared a similar story of his life. He was making the money he always wanted, but he was spending what he hoped to be making tomorrow. The problem was that his income the next month never caught up with last month's spending. The next thing you know, Dave was in bankruptcy. Fortunately, Dave was motivated enough to make a heroic change in his life. He changed his mind and his behavior completely. He did a 180-degree turn.

Dave realized what we all should: Our mental state is the core reason we allow "things" to get in our way of living a life of freedom. When we get our minds right, we can then begin to alter our behaviors. We gain freedom, clarity and, in Dave's case, financial peace. Hence the reason he calls his study Financial Peace University.

If you saw the 1987 movie, Wall Street, with Charlie Sheen and Michael Douglas, you probably remember the line where Sheen's character (Bud Fox) asks Douglas' character (Gordon Gecko) "How many yachts can you ski behind." The idea was that he was buying the same items over and over again. The next purchase was just bigger than the previous.

You see, Bud Fox aspired to be like that of Gordon Gecko. In his grand attempt to be like Gecko, he realized that Gecko was not who he really desired to be. Fox modified his behavior at the end of the movie; however, due to breaking federal laws to achieve his fortunes before his change, the consequences were detrimental.

Some questions to ask yourself

On your next drive around town, make a mental note of the junky yards and lots around you. Does the junk raise the value of the property or lower it? Think about what junk does to your life.

What items in your closet, attic, garage, or storage-unit have you attributed significance to? If it is significant enough to keep, then why is it out of sight?

If you determine success is all about the right home and the right car sitting the right neighborhood, keep this Dave Ramsey quote in mind. "Success is a pile of failure that you are standing on."

Chapter 5

The Junk Association

I do a lot of work with associations all across the country. I have been fortunate to work with the Mortgage Bankers Association, The National Restaurant Association, Associated Builders and Contractors, Trucking Association, and a myriad of other associations around the United States. I have, however, never worked with the Self-Storage Association. After you see the numbers, you'll say I should be working with the Self-Storage Association.

When I came across this self-storage facility in the middle of a tiny town, I decided to research just how many such facilities were out there. Were they successful? Did they make money? What I found out shocked me. My company conducts a lot of research on opportunities, issues, and industries. I speak nationwide on areas that include corporate university design, educational-based marketing, entrepreneurship, and sales and people development. The research I found blew me away.

I'll start with this: If you built a self-storage facility in the last ten or fifteen years, you were smart. You found one of the greatest returns for a piece of real estate and this property will keep providing income for a long time. When I called a self-storage facility to see how well they were doing, the lady told me she had five rentals left. That was five out of four hundred units that were available for rent. I recently stopped in and met a nice, older lady who owned over one thousand units with her husband near Clemson, South Carolina. I asked her how things were going in the down economy of 2010. She said they were down but still had eighty percent of their units rented.

The self-storage association website was gracious enough to provide some industry statistics that will support one of my theories, which is: We have a problem buying more than our homes will hold. The amount of stuff we own exceeds the livable square footage.

From their site, the Self Storage Association (SSA) states:

"The SSA represents the huge U.S. self-storage industry that is comprised of some 50,000 facilities. The SSA estimates that in 2009 the industry had total sales of more than $22 billion. The average U.S. self-storage facility has approximately 46,200 square feet of rentable space."

By my calculation, the amount of self-storage facilities in the U.S. is equal to 88 square miles. In case you need a way to visualize just how big that is, the District of Columbia is a mere 68 square miles.

The SSA website also goes on to state, "revenue averages $444,000 per facility or $9.52 of gross annual revenue per rentable square foot (the mean average). Nearly one in ten U.S. households, or 10% (10.8 million of the 113.3 million U.S. households in 2007) currently rent a self-storage unit; that has increased from 1 in 17 U.S. households (6%) in 1995 – an increase of approximately 65 percent in the last 15 years."

Did you get that? One in ten households rent a self-storage unit. Eighty-nine percent of all counties in the U.S. have at least one self-storage unit. That is 2,634 out of 3,141 counties. A self-storage unit, for commercial real estate development, has had one of the highest returns on investment of all commercial property. Thus, if you own some commercial property that is bare, I have a suggestion: Put a self-storage unit on it.

Here is the killer statistic. There are an estimated 58,000 self-storage facilities in the world and 50,000 of them are in the U.S. Hmmm. What does that say about us? What does that say about you, if you are that one in ten with the junk unit? What other areas of our lives should we begin to go through that are "storage areas?" What do we need to begin throwing out that we really don't need?

Okay, enough statistics. I hope I have proved my point about the seriousness of our problem. If you agree that the majority of items stored in these storage units is junk, this means we have eighty-eight square miles of it splattered across the nation. I would say it is equal to the junk on the sixty-eight square miles in the District of Columbia. I won't try to make a reference to the potential amount of junk that needs to be thrown out in DC.

There is a place in scripture, Luke 12, where Jesus uses a parable that involves storehouses. In the parable, the rich farmer had a great year in the harvest. So good, he says that, he must "tear down my barns and build bigger ones." Luke 12:18 He sounds a lot like Gordon Gecko, doesn't he?

The rich farmer in Luke 12 needed a bigger place to store the overage. He needed some self-storage units. However, what was proper for him to do in that place and time was to share with his neighbors the abundance he had received. Not only does he need storage for his harvest, he needs storage for his "goods." This is evidently the by-product of receiving so much in harvest that he can buy other items, which will presumably become junk. If you disagree with this, just think about an expensive item you have purchased. If you don't use it and take care of it, the item will wither away. Take a home sitting vacant for example. Today, with all the foreclosures around us, look at all the homes sitting empty. These homes are rotting away right in front of our eyes.

Instead of sharing with neighbors in need, the rich farmer shouts aloud, "And I'll say to myself, you have plenty of good things laid up for many years. Take life easy; eat, drink, and be merry." What a cocky, self-serving ... I'll stop there because when we get right down to it, don't we do the same thing? We may not shout out loud "I am the man and check out all I have done," but we think this way.

We have so much abundance in our personal storehouses that we go out and rent storage units or barns, as the rich farmer did. We have filled every room to the brim. The following questions need to be addressed in our lives daily. They are:

- Is the inability to release items of "insignificance" weighing us down?
- What is the root cause for holding on to things of no value and clutter in our lives?
- Can we change?

Dr. Marla Deibler, of the Center for Emotional Health in Philadelphia, wrote an article for *Metropolitan Organizing* where she states that while hoarding has the similarities of an addiction, it is not considered an addiction. She makes four key points on her blog. She states:

1. Hoarding is not an addiction; it does not involve tolerance or physiological dependence and if the behavior were to cease, there would be no physical withdrawal symptoms.

2. Hoarding is primarily driven by the strong urge to reduce or avoid anxiety or distress, whereas drug addiction is primarily driven by a desire for a "high."

3. Treatment of addiction and compulsive hoarding share commonalities, but differ significantly.

4. Individuals who compulsively hoard must engage in the process of sorting through their possessions themselves in order to be able to achieve long-term behavior change.

Dr. Deibler states that compulsion is, "behavior typically enacted in order to reduce anxiety and distress or to avoid experiencing such anxiety or distress, although common use of the word simply refers to the urge." An addiction is, "a neurobiological disorder that involves a repeated behavior (e.g., drug use) despite negative consequences, tolerance, and the experience of physical withdrawal symptoms."

The key take-home for me to encourage my friends whose spouses hoard is definitely focused on the fourth item. My friends need to help their spouses sort through all their things a little bit at a time. As you'll see later in another doctor's research, you can't just go in and begin throwing it all out for them. The emotional attachment to these items will create high stress levels and not only hurt them, but your marriage.

Dr. Dan Shoultz, a clinical psychologist I know personally in Columbia said, "Someone who hoards will need behavioral help to identify the strategies and tactics for not hoarding, but more importantly, they will need psychological help to understand and change the compulsion to hold on to things. They will need to address the fear of losing things or not being in control."

Just to show you how crazy people get who keep an abundance of items of insignificance (junk) in their lives, just catch a glimpse (this is all you'll need) of the A&E show called *Hoarders*. The show chronicles the lives of families struggling with hoarding. The families seen in this show are on the farthest end of the spectrum, as far as junk is concerned. They are so out of control, their lives are in a crisis. Just watching the show gives me the heebie jeebies.

How the show's producers even find out about the homes featured blows my mind. The families featured work with the support of a trained professional who helps them to make progress with letting go of their junk. They need a real psychologist for some of these folks. Then, a professional organizer is brought in to help the hoarder organize those items of significance left behind. Then 1-800-Got Junk comes in, gathers the junk, and takes it away. When the time comes to take the excess away, this company rummages through it in order to recycle or donate as much as possible. What can't be salvage is hauled off to the landfill. We'll talk more about landfills later.

The lifestyles portrayed on the hoarding show are extreme. Our life of holding onto physical items probably has no comparison to those folks. However, if we look closely, but in a different light, don't we hold onto emotional junk in our lives? Think about what this type of hoarding does to us. Like the hoarders, we need some sort of therapy to help us to deal with the clutter in our heads.

Some questions to ask yourself

The Self-storage Association states that roughly 50,000 of the 58,000 self-storage businesses are located in the United States. What does that say about our culture?

In a recent conversation with a life-long resident of the United Kingdom, who happens to be a world traveler, I asked him what stood out most about the United States compared to other countries. He stated, "American's have the biggest homes." Why do you think that is?

Many psychologist, even the ones interviewed for this book, state that many of their patients come to them with issues resulting from their past experiences. What past experiences are holding you back?

Chapter 6

Your Garage has a Golf Cart?

Once you notice a certain something in life, as you move that one item begins to become more and more visible, but sometimes in different ways. Here was my next self-storage encounter. However, this time, it was in my friend's neighborhood.

My good friend lives in a fairly new neighborhood not far from our home. There are nice homes, paved sidewalks, lighting, and a manicured entrance. This is probably the "typical" neighborhood built in the last fifteen years by the larger-scale developers. As I was driving to his home one Saturday, I noticed something that had totally escaped me in all my previous visits. Many of his neighbors can't park their cars in their double-car garages. If you go through the entire neighborhood, as I did, it appeared that less than 50 percent actually park their cars in their garages.

I am a car guy, even though I drive an American crossover vehicle. I really take notice when a nice vehicle is sitting out in the hot sun, especially when it's right in front of a garage door. I scratch my head when I see a beautiful vehicle, which cost more than $45,000, sitting in the driveway while a garage full of boxes occupies the space. Surely what is in those boxes doesn't exceed $45,000? Ironically, these boxes are probably the same boxes from this family's move into the home several years ago. They still sit unpacked. What the heck is in those boxes that would necessitate taking up such a valuable space? You can assume either they don't know there is a self-storage unit around the corner, or the unit they already own is full.

As my good friend always tells me, when I put my mind to something, "watch out." Here is what I did. I parked my car in the street. I was going on a neighborhood walk to see how many homes did not use their garages for parking their cars.

There wasn't any room in one driveway due to a pickup truck, Suburban, and a boat occupying the entire driveway. I recalled this boat has been sitting waiting for refurbishment for the last two years. From the street, I looked to see what is in this garage? Well, let's see what's in there. Two sawhorses holding up some piece of material from a woodworking project (apparently still awaiting the final details), two four-wheelers, skateboard ramps, and other miscellaneous items. Oh, and we can't forget the lawn mower and other yard instruments.

Have you ever been out in the country around Halloween and walked through a corn maze? They are actually fun and the kids love it. Well, that is what I feel like when I walk through this garage. There is no straight line from the garage door to the kitchen door.

I decided to walk the entire neighborhood. What I noticed was the first home was very similar to all the other homes in the neighborhood. What really blew me away is that this neighborhood is a small neighborhood compared to those mammoth residential neighborhoods in Duluth and Alpharetta that actually require a visitor to use a GPS to navigate through. I bet Congress has contemplated making them our 51st and 52nd states in the union. This neighborhood is small enough that you can walk it entirely in 15 minutes. Why do I address the size of the neighborhood? Guess what many of the garages had parked inside? Answer: a golf cart. I am talking about an $8,000 golf cart that is Clemson orange with tiger paws all over it. Some golf carts looked like they were upcoming entrants into the next Monster Truck race at the coliseum. These golf carts had flames, eyes, and were jacked up like a monster truck so much that a stepladder may be required to get in.

So why the heck would you need a golf cart to get to your neighbor's house? You can't drive them on our streets with our city ordinances. The word we need to focus on is "significance." A new golf cart has a significant price tag, but does it have significance to our life? Do you find significance in circling the neighborhood with a Corona and Kenny Chesney blasting on the golf cart radio?

When I had my 118-acre farm outside of Camden, SC, I owned a Kawasaki Mule. The mule is a four-wheeled, off-road vehicle similar to a golf cart. It was used as both a work vehicle for me and a toy for my kids. You can't roam the woods in a pickup. One low hanging tree limb can cause $2,000 plus in damage, or a pointed stump will force you to acquire a new $400 tire. When I decided to sell the farm, I actually sold the mule first for exactly what I had paid for it 2 years earlier. When I decided to sell the farm, the significance of the mule was gone. I don't need it on my tiny .8-acre lot.

What junk is occupying your garage? Think about what is really significant in your life. Where is it and when is the last time you used it? Many people have shared that their significant items are easily accessible or close to them. Ever see a family going through the debris after a fire? They go to specific areas where their most precious items were left or stored. Regretfully, you hear story after story from those who have experienced such a tragedy that every physical item is replaceable. Many simply want to recover items like wedding albums, kids albums, and videos of their treasured memories.

As I researched all the junk we have in our lives, many people I met across the country shared stories about their junk. It was interesting to hear a couple's opinion of junk. In virtually all conversations, there was one spouse who liked to keep everything and one spouse who desired to get rid of it. Can you guess which spouse ususally won? Story upon story was shared about holding one to certain items that were sure to be needed or valuable some day in the future. So, when will that be? The one good thing to note in all the stories shared, we all smiled or laughed about our habitual nature of buying, finding, and keeping.

One story shared by a husband was typical. He chimed in with "it's her junk, not mine!" His wife had this obsession with going out every Saturday morning to see what treasure she could find at a yard sale or the local flea market. Almost always, she will come home with some item. After years of searching and buying, the couple had to rent a self storage unit because the home and garage were too full. Does this sound like someone you know?

Here is a simple exercise. Go outside and open your garage door from the outside. Answer these questions honestly.

I can park two cars in my garage.	Excellent
I can park one car in my garage.	Good Job
I can't park my cars in the garage, but I can walk to my door with ease.	Not bad
I can't park my cars, nor can I walk easily to the door of my home.	Bad
I can't see my door.	You need help

Most garages, with the cars parked outside, are obstacle courses for anyone to get through. Next time you are in your garage, make a mental inventory of what you have. Have you used an item in the last six months or even a year? If not, think about what you can do with it. Could it be donated, sold or given away to someone in need? And, for those boxes still taped from when you moved into your home, open them up and see what surprise you might find. In all likelihood, you'll find that missing item you've looked for the last few years, or you'll find some items that the mission downtown could surely use.

When you clear the paths of your garage, you'll find freedom and a place to park your car(s). Imagine cleaning out the clutter in your life. What would that look like? What would happen? Think about the freedom and clarity you will find in your life once you removed all the obstacles. You will experience life in a totally different light.

Think back to the clutter I discussed in my personal life when doctors found my tumor. You couldn't walk a straight line through my own life due to all the junk I had brought in. I had to personally weave in and out of my days, much like these garages, in order to get from one place to another. I lived on a schedule, and I had no freedom. If someone needed my help or a visit, I couldn't even spare an hour in that week due to the junk in my life. My life had become the crowded double-car garage. I needed a large personal self-storage unit to put my junk in. The tumor was a wake up call for me.

Regretfully, the junk between my ears was probably greater than the boxes in those garages in my friend's neighborhood. It is amazing the number of people who have echoed that sentiment in the last year. They have missed out on opportunities with their spouses, children, and friends due to being obstructed by insignificant agendas and acquisitions in their life. The American Dream has lost its gleam.

Some questions to ask yourself

If you have a golf cart parked in your garage, here are two questions for you:

1. *Is the amount you paid for the golf cart equal to or less than the amount of money you have invested for your child(s) education fund?*

2. *Is the amount you paid for the golf cart equal to or less than the amount of money you have invested in your retirement account?*

Can you park your car in your garage? If no, then what is taking up that space? Is the value of the item(s) equal to (or greater than) the value of your car?

Chapter 7

Your Inheritance is Their Junk

We were at a dinner one evening and they had heard about my research into the junk in our lives. One couple addressed the situation in their life, but with a different perspective. One of the ladies gave us some insight into her in-law's current home situation. They owned a 3,000 square foot home, with four spacious bedrooms, a double car garage, and a storage shed in the backyard. All the children had moved out within the last three years so it was just the in-laws in the home. With this much room and only two people occupying this space, her in-laws still needed to rent a self-storage unit for all of their furniture that just wouldn't fit "comfortably" into the home any longer. They were willing to remove the clutter from their home, but they couldn't remove the clutter from their lives. We all inquired if they were saving the furniture for the kids to use later as they moved into new, larger homes. "This isn't the furniture that we'd want to put in our homes," she answered. Then she added, "I guess they'll just pay $90-plus a month for climate-controlled storage units for the rest of their lives."

Immediately after she made this statement, the floodgates opened with more conversation about our parents' slightly, if ever used, stuff that we didn't want, and they refused to part with. The concern by most at the table was the amount of time and energy it would take for us to sell, donate, or throw away our parents' things when they passed away or were moved into a retirement facility. How long would it take to deal with all of these things, not counting the probate work to account for every item? Just think about all the items your parents attribute significance to that will most likely end up being sold at an estate auction or yard sale. Each of their children's homes are already full of their possessions. If Ashley and I were to take simply a couple of pieces of furniture from my parents' homes, we'd have to remove similar furniture from ours. Knowing this, the only sure bet is an estate auction or a large, climate-controlled storage unit.

I recently joked with my parents that when they went off to heaven, I was going to have a big yard sale and put a sign in the yard advertising everything for a dollar. You can imagine the look my mom gave me. It may not be sold for a dollar, but I can assure you it will be one good sale. Honestly, what are we supposed to do with all these things when the time comes to sell our parents' home? My home, like yours, is already full. I am an only child. My dad's garage is full of tools and I have no room to put them in mine. I have a small 6x6 foot shed full of my own yard tools. He has a 20 x 15-foot workshop with every tool imaginable.

My neighbor recently lost both his parents within a six-month time span. Unexpectedly, here he was dealing with the loss of his parents as well as the loads of estate work that soon followed. I remember my parents going through the details when their parents died, but their estates were simple and much smaller. My neighbor's parents had done well financially, therefore requiring more work of my neighbor. The amount of work was more that I would have imagined. I don't want you to think the amount of work in dealing with the estate exceeded the pain he felt in the loss. It simply didn't. However, we fail to realize the enormity of work required after death in order to get things "in order." If things like properly deeded property, correct beneficiaries on insurance policies, savings accounts, and the will are not in order, then probate will seemingly go on forever.

Thankfully, my friend's parents had downsized from a beautiful lake home to a two-bedroom home within five miles of their home just two years prior to their deaths. In that move, they sold the boat, all the items from the third bedroom and cleaned out their garage and attic. Even with that advance purging, it took hours upon hours to sell, donate and throw away those things from his parents' two bedroom home. I know, because I helped.

His parents had seen that those items of past significance had no real significance at the end of their lives. They helped my friend in having their house in order as well as all the other details associated with their life. I went with my neighbor to get the items from his father's nursing home a few days after his death. Having a pickup provides many opportunities to serve in your neighborhood. There was a soberness about the fact that the few things his father would utilize in his last days all fit into my pickup. This included his recliner, TV, small dresser, nightstand, light and pictures of his children and grandchildren. Everything fit perfectly into a standard pickup.

In a New York Times article "When Possessions Lead to Paralysis," Paula Span writes a great article on the physical and emotional impact our possessions can have on older generations. In her interview with Dr. David J. Ekerdt, University of Kansas Director of the Gerontology Center, she writes of the different ways the older generations can begin to remove the significant and insignificant things from their lives in order to give more freedom to children in the later years of life. She writes, "The sheer volume of objects in a typical household, the enormous physical and cognitive effort involved in sorting out what's essential, the psychological toll of parting with what's disposable — all can lead to a kind of paralysis that keeps seniors in place, even when the place isn't the best place." Because we don't attribute the same significance to our parent's things that they do, when we go to remove these things, it causes emotional stress to our parents. We must be careful when removing, but that should not stop us from removing the lesser things of value.

"This isn't just a move from one residence to another, as it would be earlier in life. This is a step closer to the inevitable world of frail aging, and a reminder that time is growing short. People want to hold on to the symbols of their former lives and competence," Ekerdt told the Times. The key is to respect the belongings of your parents and obtain their approval before removing the clutter from both of your lives. If our elders can take control of their many possessions and remove them from their lives by giving or selling, the burden is removed from both parents and their children long-term.

Just last week, my family and I visited a neighbor who had been widowed and now sat in the nursing home under hospice care. When hospice is called in, you are near the end of life. The wonderful job of hospice is to see that those who are in their last days die with dignity and the least amount of pain. This neighbor was celebrating her last birthday, and we wanted to just love on her. Pause and think about this. What present do you bring a person in her last days for a birthday present. The only answer is love. We laughed as she reminisced about all the things she had witnessed our kids doing in those years we lived near each other.

She had lived down the street from us in a home on the lake. In her home were beautiful handmade quilts, porcelain vases from Rome, and many beautiful items she and her husband had acquired over a forty-year marriage. However, in the end, she has only a few things in a room that measures 400 square feet. Her room has a few items that could be carried out in one wheel barrel. Here at the end of her life, she keeps the things most precious to her by her bed. This includes a Bible, several pictures of her dog and crayon drawings from children who love her. That is it. To many, these are insignificant things, but to her they are extremely significant to her. As scripture says, "We come into this world with nothing and we leave with nothing."

As I get older, the funerals of my friends' parents are becoming more and more frequent. Seeing their many years of effort in providing for their family, the words of the Ecclesiastical writer stand out.

"I denied myself nothing my eyes desired;

    I refused my heart no pleasure.

My heart took delight in all my work,

    and this was the reward for all my labor.

Yet when I surveyed all that my hands had done

    and what I had toiled to achieve,

everything was meaningless, a chasing after the wind;

nothing was gained under the sun." Ecclesiastes 2:10-11

Some questions to ask yourself

What items in your home are you holding onto for your children (or family member) to inherit? Do they really want it? If it is that important…give it away now.

When you die, what will happen with the majority of the items in your possession? Remember, you can't take them with you.

Read Ecclesiastes Chapter 2 and meditate on what he is speaking about.

Chapter 8

Sports Junkies

When the fall season begins, the hysteria of college and professional football begins to set in as well. In the South, college football games are where you'll find families huddled around cars tailgating and enjoying their Saturdays. For many of those families, they will spend at least seven days away from their homes to attend their team's home football games. When you count four season tickets, parking, club membership, and food, my friends tell me they are spending between $3,000 and $5,000 per year. The devotion and preparation for each game has to weigh on the family. The priorities made during these sport's seasons has a tremendous effect on families.

This past October, a front-page article in our state's paper tried to present a humorous story about a father's love for his college football team. Regretfully, the article was a sad example of a father's priorities being sorely out of place.

The article focused on a young girl, who had been making plans for a wedding during the month of October. The writer tells us that the young girl approached her dad just prior to football season, evidently not thinking of anything but her wedding day, in order to finalize her wedding date. You can imagine the excitement of the moment. She and her fiancé had probably spent hours combing through dates in order to pick the very best one. So when she brought the date to her father, his very first reaction was to pull out his wallet in order to check the football schedule. In doing this, he saw that his team would be playing a home game that day and told his daughter the wedding will interrupt his and her brother's schedule that day. What he was really telling her was that his football game meant more than his daughter's most precious day. This is a great example of some sports-crazed fathers in America. We will actually put football games ahead of our anniversaries, birthdays, and weddings. The only question the reporter didn't ask the father was if he also carried a picture of his daughter in his wallet?

When Ashley and I selected the date for our wedding, here are the two things that entered our decision. One, she wanted to be finished with her doctoral program in pharmacy. Two, we wanted an anniversary date around a federal holiday that would give us long weekends for celebrating the rest of our lives. We selected Labor Day weekend. Now if you are into college football, you know this is generally the first weekend game for many college teams. Here is our marriage story.

Both of my in-laws went to Georgia. Most of my family went to the University of South Carolina. Growing up, Ashley spent many Saturdays in Athens, and I spent many Saturdays at Williams-Brice Stadium, the home of the Gamecocks. Guess who played on September 2, 1995.. You guessed it, the Georgia Bulldogs played the University of South Carolina in Columbia. Of course, our families let us know what we had done, and we let them know they didn't have to come. We had our wedding and everyone lived. One funny scene from our wedding video is when the camera, high up in the balcony, pans to show the entire audience, and my Uncle Max and Uncle Jimmy are watching a hand-held television during the ceremony. We still get a kick out of that every time we watch the video. They, and many of our attendees, were season ticket holders at South Carolina and Georgia. We know we meant more to them than their ball teams.

It used to be that little league sports went year-round with generally three sports: baseball, basketball, and football. Today, little league teams play one sport all year long. There are traveling teams where the family travels many times a month to some tournament in another city. Often times, this requires a family to live out of hotel rooms and spend all day at the ballpark. Doesn't this sound more like pro sports than little league?

Many sports are willing to make this sacrifice in the hopes that their child gets that full-ride to a Division I school. Many have dreams that their sons and daughters can make it to the "big leagues." The reality is that less than 2% of all high school athletes ever make it to the pros. According to the NCAA, there were over 900,000 high school seniors eligible to play at any level of NCAA in 2010. For you parents investing all your time and money either living out your kid's dreams or even your dreams, these statistics from the NCAA may dampen your spirit.

Student Athletes

	Men's Basketball	Women's Basketball	Football	Baseball	Men's Ice Hockey	Men's Soccer
High School Seniors	155,756	127,088	317,801	135,801	10,644	109,664
Freshman Roster Positions	4,832	4,395	18,537	8,519	1,172	6,172
% To play NCAA (all levels)	3%	3.5%	5.8%	6.3%	11%	5.6%

http://www.ncaa.org/wps/wcm/connect/public/NCAA/Resources/Basketball+Resources/Basketball+Resource+Probability+of+Going+Pro

With an estimated 40 million kids playing youth sports today, many families have made this investment, only to see their children burn out or even get hurt to the point they can't play competitively any longer. I have seen families invest weekends upon weekends in order for their child to make it to a Division I school, but when they get only Division II offers for a free ride in college, they turn these offers down. What has been significant for the family in the last ten years is now all gone. The part of the family I feel sorry for is the sibling(s) of the star player, as they have to go from city to city, weekend after weekend, sitting through game after game. What are we telling those kids? Are we literally saying, "Your big brother is more important than you are right now?" With love and care in my voice, I tell my friends living this lifestyle the following: "Family time ain't at the ballpark."

I would say that this lifestyle requires a good look in the mirror.

It may possibly work for some, but ultimately the cost must be counted. We need to redefine the purpose of the family first, and then consider sports. We have allowed the guardrails around the family and the church to simply be removed, thus allowing our little league and high school coaches to dictate our family schedules. If the family would weigh the consequences of these decisions, things could change. Couldn't we go back to one practice per week and one game a week? We could go back to Sunday worship and Sunday rest. It is no wonder we are continually worn out and depressed. It is no wonder our kids have to take medications to have focus in school. The last questions are very simple ones: Do your children get to enjoy being children? Do you, as a parent, get to enjoy being a parent versus being their manager? Or, are sports just another form of junk in your life? Does your life hinge on how teenagers perform during the Saturday game?

Some questions to ask yourself

Do you give more time and money to an athletic program than you do the church or organizations that serve widows, orphans, or the homeless?

Do you spend more hours at the ballpark than hours with the family at dinner?

Are your children being pushed to live out your dreams of success on the field or court?

Chapter 9

Junk Mind and Body

Have you ever thought about those actions and attitudes you said you would NEVER do because you saw your mom and dad doing them? Whatever these things were, they drove you crazy. You'd run in your room, close the door and scream, "I will never do that" or "I'll never be like that." Then twenty years later, you look in the mirror and say, "I can't believe I just did that." Outside of our credit card debt, think of how much personal stuff we brought into our marriages. This garbage includes everything from past girlfriend/boyfriend relationships to our lack of achievement in college or our first jobs.

In talking with two psychologists who I know personally and who are leading clinical psychologist in Columbia, they both have seen years of bad decisions and heartache wreck the lives of not only individuals but families. I interviewed these men to see how "junk" in our past affects our ability to live today and even into tomorrow. Junk, in this context, is bad memories, failure to forgive, and failed relationships. I explicitly asked them to avoid discussing things like the effects of child and spousal abuse when talking about our inability to live life to its fullest potential. This type of abuse is inflicted by someone else and will inevitably create trauma long-term.

Dr. Tom Barbian, another clinical psychologist I know in Columbia, told me that many of the issues treated in their facility indeed stem from events in the past. "The past shapes our development," he stated, "and our development determines who we become ... who we are." As we talked about dealing with our past, knowing there are so many events that could have impacted each of us, he mentioned that even our biochemical makeup could shift due to our past.

A statement we can all agree on is that we can "be in bondage to our past." Letting the past go and not allowing it to shape who you are can be very difficult. The past becomes the junk in our minds that tell us the direction we should take, even though we know we shouldn't. Our mental garage becomes cluttered and our paths become filled with more obstacles.

When I went into greater detail with Dr. Barbian as to my research on the overuse of drugs to cope with painful situations, versus clinical therapy, he stated that in many cases drugs only offer a temporary fix. These issues will continue to resurface if not addressed with therapy or therapy with medication. Therapy is the best approach to getting to the root cause of our problems.

Not surprisingly, both men clearly stated that our difficulty in dealing with events of our past become mental roadblocks in our lives. Whether it is living through a divorce as a child or your failed marriage, the past can have a huge impact on who you are today and tomorrow. If we allow these events to impair our judgment and decision-making ability, then we allow them to rob us of our opportunities and relationships. Isn't it worth dealing with the past today so that we can be freed?

Another psychologist, Dr. Shoultz, told me the greatest instance of junk he sees in his patients is selfishness. He stated, "The junk I see is mostly selfishness. We are significantly affected by our personal wants and perceived needs." Dr. Shoultz believes that selfishness is moderated by the effects of society and our family experiences. He said, "The effect of our parents is the largest effect I see upon people, effecting 40% to 50% of why we do things."

The most regretful item I found in my research is that our society turns too quickly to medication and too late to therapy. Not only do we rely on these quick fixes for our depression, we turn to medication for dealing with problems such as weight, smoking, high blood pressure and many other issues physically. These medications are not treating the root cause or the real problem.

Junk in our minds and in our bodies may be the greatest hindrance to finding the freedom to live and the enjoyment life can bring. This behavior impacts our ability to look at a situation properly and see its intrinsic value. You could say it is like seeing the glass half empty versus half full. That gray matter between your ears has a lot to do with who you are and whether you have a willingness to change a behavior.

American's statistics on prescription and over-the-counter drug use is staggering. According to a study by Medco Health Solutions, a company that manages prescription drug benefits, more than 50 percent of people in the U.S. are now taking at least one drug for chronic health problem, while twenty percent are taking three or more. Another study, conducted by the nonprofit Henry J. Kaiser Family Foundation, found that the number of prescriptions purchased in the U.S. increased 71 percent between 1994 and 2005, from 2.1 billion to 3.6 billion (a 58% increase). In contrast, the U.S. population grew by only 9 percent.

The U.S. Centers for Disease Control and Prevention, commonly referred to as the CDC, indicates about 130 million Americans ingest prescribed medication every month. Americans consume more medicine per person than any other country. The number of prescriptions has increased by two-thirds over the past decade to 3.5 billion yearly, according to IMS Health, a pharmaceutical consulting company. From the polling results, we even take more nonprescription drugs.

Why has there been such an increase in taking medications? Look at what the CDC states in their report. "One reason for the surge in prescriptions is that people's health is actually getting worse, largely due to lifestyle diseases." Again, obesity and popping pills goes back to "lifestyle" diseases. What is a lifestyle disease? I say it is the junk in our lives that we allow to exist that prevents us from living life fully. Lifestyle diseases include heart disease, stroke, obesity, and type-2 diabetes. These diseases could be caused by smoking, drugs, and an abundance of alcohol. The statement given as to what helps eliminate "lifestyle disease" is quite simple. Consistent physical activity helps prevent lifestyle diseases and premature mortality.

"Americans have had an increase in the incidence of obesity, which can lead to all kinds of health problems," said Dr. Lon Castle, Medco's Senior Director of the Department of Medical and Analytical Affairs. "They also have a penchant for going for the quick fix. They want medications to treat their problems rather than trying diet and exercise or lifestyle changes, which might also be effective."

We Americans want quick fixes to our problems, instead of working them out day by day. We don't go to the doctor looking for answers. We go to the doctor looking for a quick fix. We have developed bad habits, which have either grown in size or become more frequent. Before long, the problems begin to surface until they are so burdensome, we must seek medical attention.

For obesity, the buffet lines and fast food restaurants have encouraged our over-eating habits. Fast food restaurants and the creation of the extra-large value meal is one of the biggest reasons for the exponential growth of obesity in our children. We are surrounded by food that is unhealthy and portions large enough for two meals, rather than one.

So what about the cost of obesity? The CDC states the following as it relates to the physical costs: "Obesity is a costly condition that can reduce quality of life and increase the risk for many serious chronic diseases and premature death." Obesity is not just the junk we put in our mouths, it is our lack of exercise. The Charleston's *Post and Courier* in a September 2010 front-page article stated, "South Carolina has one of the highest obesity rates in the county, a growing problem that leaves many with multiple medical problems and costs the state more than $1 billion each year." This is a good example of the monetary cost to our society. In CDC published a report stating that, "From 1987 to 2001, diseases associated with obesity accounted for 27% of the increases in U.S. medical costs. For 2006, medical costs associated with obesity were estimated at as much as $147 billion (in 2008 dollars); among all payers, obese persons had estimated medical costs that were $1,429 higher than persons of normal weight."

On a monthly basis, an overweight person costs $120 more a month than a typical or healthy person. The worst news is that in the future this will result in even higher costs. Our young kids and teens will exceed all current generations in obesity; therefore, healthcare costs will rise.

Relationships can be severely affected by junk in our past. The more I talk with psychologists, the more I realize that how we were raised and the events in our lives shape who we become. It may be how your dad treated your mom. Maybe it is how your mom responded when angry. It is amazing how many little things shape our lives so significantly. Ultimately, what is coming out is in your heart, and you must work to protect your heart. It is the wellspring of life.

In Proverbs 4:23, Solomon, the wisest and richest man in the history of the world writes, "Above all else, guard your heart, for everything you do flows from it." A wellspring is a source of continual supply. In this context, it is a continual supply of emotions. When Solomon wrote these words, their culture believed that the heart, rather than the brain, was the source of human wisdom. It was our emotions and our personality. So what is in your wellspring? As Judy Rushfeldt, author and creator of lifetoolsforwomen.com, "Your heart will define your attitudes, beliefs, thoughts, and choices -- ultimately, they mold your destiny."

We see the effects of not protecting our hearts in failed marriages, struggling marriages, and dysfunctional families. In the U.S., we lead the world with 4.95 divorces per 1,000 people (not marriages). Husbands and fathers must see that protecting their hearts, as well as their marriages and families, as top priorities. It is above providing financially for your family; that, for most men, is hard to understand. If we men don't protect our hearts, and ultimately our marriages, the statics prove that our children will follow suit.

I want to end this chapter on a positive note regarding junk in our bodies and minds. In January 1970, when I was only three years old, my mom began experiencing blood clots in her leg. This was junk in her body that she did not intentionally put there, but junk, none the less, that was causing havoc to her body. Without diving into too many details, the result was to amputate her toes. Within months, the clotting issues resurfaced. The next choice was to amputate her foot. As before, months would pass and the symptoms would persist. The logical next option was to amputate her leg below the knee in July 1970. Thankfully, three surgeries in a seven-month span, and over fifty days in the hospital, the clotting problems finally went away. In all that time, she never let it get her down.

My mom is a great example of a person not letting past junk dictate her life. She could have easily taken a different route at the age of thirty-four when she lost her leg. She didn't. She committed herself to getting back up, and with a positive attitude, literally ran through her physical therapy. A few years later, she would run with me, while teaching me to ride a bike. Four years later, she taught me to properly punt and kick a football. That year, I would go on to win Kershaw's Punt, Pass, and Kick competition and place third in the county competition.

Today, most of my friends have no idea she is an amputee. She never complains and never slows down. Her example in my life and the lives of my children continue to inspire us each day to move forward without complaint. How we handle life after a humiliating event or circumstance is ultimately up to us. Don't allow physical and emotional junk to determine who you are. If it requires therapy, then be true to yourself and get help. If it requires a determination to overcome, knowing there will be setbacks, charge forward.

"As iron sharpens iron, so one person sharpens another."

Proverbs 27:17

Some questions to ask yourself

What junk do you carry around between your ears?

What junk do you carry around your belt?

Which relationships are you jeopardizing because you lack professional help?

Chapter 10

Take My Junk Away

As we begin to look at how to clean out our homes, one company I came across during my research may be of benefit to you. This company has over two hundred franchisees around the United States and Canada. Their success in the junk business has given them the recognition as being one of the "Top 400" franchises in the country. 1-800-Got Junk actually comes to your home and takes your junk and trash away. They give you a quote and a date to haul. If you accept, they haul it off, and all you have to do is pay. The quote is based on the volume of things you desire to rid of. They load it up, haul it off to sort what can be recycled, and then move the remaining to the landfill. You might be asking yourself, "They make money doing that?" Well, remember the amount of items we discussed in your self-storage units. It appears that while we've covered more than our nation's capital with stuff in these units, we have more than that in our homes, garages, attics, and sheds.

In 1989, college student Brian Scudamore found it hard to get a job in his hometown of Vancouver, Canada. After seeing an old, junk-hauling truck driving through a local restaurant drive-thru, he made a decision to start his own business is hauling off junk. It simply began as a means to pay for his college bills. Today, 800-Got-Junk is a multi-million dollar franchise. In 2007, Scudamore was awarded the International Franchise Association's Entrepreneur of the Year. To think that Scudamore received all of this revenue and recognition for simply removing junk from peoples homes and businesses.

When I began researching the types of junk removal companies, I found something very intriguing. The way in which these companies charge for coming to your home and removing the junk that you have so honorably decided to free from your cluttered life, is not by the hour times the number of men and women it takes to remove the stuff, or the mileage to the dump, or the size of truck needed for your items. Instead the fee is based on the volume and weight of your junk. The time it takes to remove the clutter from your home or business is immaterial; what matters is the size and weight of your junk. Think about this in your own life. How much time could it possibly take you to go and begin cleaning out? If you or your neighbor don't have a pickup to haul your junk off, then you know who you can call. If your clutter is mental junk, you know it is time to call a good friend or a good therapist. Perhaps this junk is weighing you down more than you know.

Think this through with me. How much time does it take to actually determine which items need to be let go? If you walked through your garage, went up into your attic, went down to the basement, or went under the house and retrieved items that could be discarded, how long would it take? How long would it take to put your junk beside the road for the next trash pickup? How long would it take to load it in your car or your neighbor's pickup (as my friends do), in order to haul it to a consignment shop or the local mission? How long would it take to Google "800-Got-Junk" for the local franchise in order to get them to come and give you a quote? How long?

Think about how we introduce junk to our kids. Start with the kid's meal. How many meals at the McDonalds, Burger King, or other fast food restaurant put those junky toys, that are not worth five cents, in the boxes. Think about the significance of these toys to your children when ordering their meal at any of these restaurants. They don't really care about the nuggets or kid's burger, all they want to do is get the box and open up that plastic wrap and play with the plastic toy. Inevitably, when I go to clean out the car after a family trip, I have three of these ridiculous items to throw away. Each one was so important at the time of purchase, yet now sits in the floorboard of our car to simply get lost under the seat. I usually find them when I go to vacuum out the car and hear the vacuum scream when the toy gets stuck in the nozzle. I bet these junky toys are what drove the Chinese economy over the last quarter century. I know China appreciates our eating habits.

Another thought to ponder is all the junk people buy at dollar stores. "Hmm, wonder why this is only a dollar?" Well, just wait until you walk out the door of the store and your purchase falls apart in your hand. That broom, mop bucket, kitchen utensil, and especially that toy, will disintegrate in mere minutes of use. One of our family members, who comes by about three times a year, stops by one of these stores and buys our kids this junk. On the last visit, the yo-yo came completely apart (I mean broken) after the third flick of the wrist, and the paddle ball toy broke on the very first pounce. Neither could be fixed. Again, the Chinese love our purchasing of their junk.

Have you ever watched Veggie Tales? If you have, you probably saw the story of Madam Blueberry, who wants more and more and more. More of what you ask? Madame Blueberry wants MORE STUFF. Sure, she has everything she needs, but like us Americans, that are not worth five cents she wants more. She wants to be like the proverbial Joneses, the family next door. And she decides to go to "Stuff Mart" to get it. Sound familiar? Of course it does. If you want to get a good quick visual, stop reading and go online and watch this clip on YouTube.

Just like Madam Blueberry desired to have more and more stuff, the sad reality is that this is also our state of mind. We acquire items for virtually no reason at all and then it takes a pair of pliers (or death) to separate us from the stuff. Why would we intentionally continue to go and buy so many things? Why does the story of Madam Blueberry ring so true for so many of us? Why are we so enamored with acquiring items of insignificance to merely keep up with our neighbors?

If you are one of those people that likes to shop or just go buy things, here is an idea. Get in touch with Angel Child, the local women's shelter, or the local food bank. Buy a birthday present for someone who hasn't seen a birthday gift in years (if ever). Bring joy not only to yourself; bring long-term joy to a person who really has a need. Think of the return on that investment. It will reap years and years of rewards.

Some questions to ask yourself

So you've identified junk in your home. What will you do next?

When you go into a store, are you compelled to buy something? Are you like Madam Blueberry?

GARAGE SALE

Chapter 11

ROJ (Return on Junk)

There is no place I detest going in my home more than my attic. Bending over at a 90-degree angle or squatting like Johnny Bench is undesirable. Thankfully, I only go up there about three times a year. Of course all of our Christmas ornaments are in the attic, so I spend more time up there during Christmas than any other time.

However, this year, I had to walk up those stairs a few more times. With our children moving up in age, we decided that it was time for the yard sale or "junk sale" as I call it. When junk begins to fill the shelves in my garage and it becomes difficult to get out of my car when I pull into my garage, I know the time has come. When I look underneath my covered deck or the crawl space under the house and see things I did not know I owned, I know it is time for the big sale.

As kids grow older, those large plastic toys acquired either through the toy store or a neighbor's handoff, take up a lot of room. It's the basketball goal, the play kitchen, bicycles, and tricycles that I am talking about. One thing that is good about kids' toys is that you will usually sell most of the items and what you don't sell can always be given to a kid in need.

When we started putting out all the items in our garage a couple of days before the sale, it took only a few hours to completely fill up the entire garage. This cleaning out included an old couch, old desk, and three old TVs. This didn't even include all the large kids toys that we left outside. Before long, we ran out of room in the garage. We then started storing our junk on the front porch. When we ran out of room there, we started filling up our dining room. Do you think we had some clutter in that home that we didn't even recognize? By 10 p.m. that night, we still hadn't finished finding all the items we wanted to sell. I looked at my wife, knowing that in a mere nine hours all chaos would erupt with the first guests arriving at 6:50 a.m., and suggested we just go to bed and finish the work in the morning. Before we went to bed, Ashley and I set a goal of $500 for all the things we didn't need any longer and were taking up space in our lives.

The next morning I got up about 5:45 to make the coffee and walk the dog. As I hooked our dog up to her leash and started out the front door, something hit me. The early garage sale shoppers could be waiting outside, even though it wasn't yet seven. This had occurred during our last yard sale a few years back. I didn't want to take any chances, so I quickly turned and went out the back door and walked around my neighbor's home to move to the street to walk the dog. As I rounded the corner, the coast was clear. No one was sitting in our driveway waiting for the sale to begin. After getting back to the house and waking up Ashley, the kids were already awake and ready for the big sale. Ashley and I were still dragging, not quite ready. The kids were bouncing off the walls, ready to push the garage door button, and shout "show me the money!"

Sure enough, after a mere two cups of coffee, out of my normal eight cups, the sale began. Within minutes, and I mean minutes, a fourth of our junk was acquired by two people in a pickup, presumably heading with our things to the flea market to sell at a higher price. Now this is something I really don't understand, but I hear they make good money doing it. We started at seven and by nine, half of the junk was gone and we had some money in our pockets.

We have had yard sales before and we learned a valuable lesson, don't put prices on anything. It is a waste of time. We were taking about any offer made on this stuff, within reason.

What I have come to realize with yard sales is that the people buying are normally packrats themselves. Here is my proof. Many of the shoppers are older folks who seem to be retired. Due to their age and health, I had to load probably thirty percent of our junk in their vehicles. In loading, inevitably I was moving junk from their previous yard sales to make room for what they had acquired from us. Now get this, I don't mean what they acquired earlier that morning at other sales, I mean from the previous Saturday. They had driven with many of the items for seven or more days in their cars. When I asked them how many garage sales they had attended prior to ours, they would laugh and say, "This is from last Saturday. You're the first today."

Being somewhat of a neat freak, my house policy for clothes is that they have only three places to reside outside of the washer and dryer. This includes the dresser drawers, hung properly in the closet, or the dirty clothes hamper. There are no other options, and the den is not where we keep our shoes. So when I loaded these items into someone's car and had to move their clothes and junk in order to load additional junk, I cringed. I used more hand sanitizer that day than normal. Unlike 800-Got-Junk, where you pay them to take it off, these kind folks were paying me and hauling it away.

We exceeded our goal of $500 by $5. We had sold $505 of junk that had occupied our garage, porches, attic, and back yard. In the end, I took our remaining items to a local ministry. It took about six hours of preparation and six hours of selling. Ashley couldn't believe that we had stored so many things around us that we really didn't need. Getting rid of our insignificant items wasn't so hard.

I have friends with wives and daughters who love to shop at the mall and feel empty if they come home empty-handed. Just like those garage sale shoppers, who feel they have to spend a dollar on something at every stop, they need professional therapy. This is an addiction called omniomania, which is the psychiatric term for compulsive shopping, or shopping addiction. People with oniomania shop on impulse as a way of coping and find it difficult to control their spending or shopping behaviors. Omniomania is perhaps the most socially reinforced of the behavioral addictions thanks to advertising, promotions, and easy access to instruments like credit cards that allow us to live outside our means. Like Dave

Ramsey says, "Act your wage."

Advertisers spend billions of dollars on billboards, magazines, internet, and television ads to encourage you to go get whatever it is you need or think you may need. Infomercials have to be the biggest gimmick on television today. If you join the Association of National Advertisers, you have immediate access to over 3,000 marketing insights and research to every buying audience in America. They spend millions each year identifying your buying habits and addictions. They know what impulses you act on, such as "act now and receive..." They know you and what moves you. Unless you turn off the television and ignore print ads, they have you in their grasp.

Much like attorneys who move to the other side of the court-room and become trial attorneys in order to make more money, our clinical psychologists have moved out of counseling offices into advertising agencies and corporations in order to get inside your mind and encourage these bad habits. If you ever heard of or remember the famed Ivan Pavlov who used conditioning to get a dog to salivate at the mere ringing of the bell, we are now conditioned to the point that we salivate during commercials and special offers. We buy and then we store in our closets, garages, and attics. We may even need a bigger home. Sickening isn't it.

Do you have garage sales or attend them?

If you had a garage sale, would you be willing to remove the items of insignificance in your home or storage unit?

If you could not sell all your items of insignificance at a garage sale, would you be willing to donate those items or simply discard those of no value?

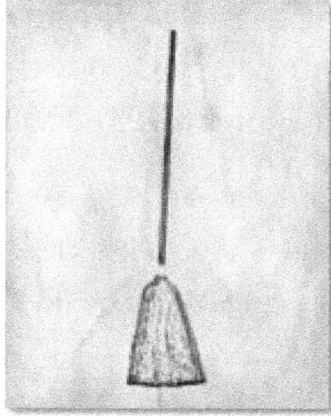

Chapter 12

The Big Clean Out

The day after I found out about the tumor in my colon, I began to list every extracurricular item in my life that existed. Immediately, I began to see my own personal junk. It wasn't in my garage or in my attic, as that area was pretty cleaned out. It was in a place where I couldn't see it. It was in my life and in my heart. As I peered inside, the question I had to ask was, "Do I really need that in here?"

What could I weed out? Growing up on a farm, you know exactly what weeds do to your crops. They choke out the items you intentionally planted and deplete your harvest. It was evident there were weeds in my life garden that needed immediate attention. I would not use herbicides (medication). I would get in and begin pulling each weed out, one at a time.

By listing out each activity, company, and commitment one-by-one, I could put it in order of priority. Once I had the order of importance, I could then start from the bottom and work my way up to the top, striking out those that did not meet my definition of "significant." As you might imagine, the top three things in my life did not need to appear on the list. These were my faith in Jesus, my wife, and my children. Those were the beautiful plants in my life that I desired to protect. As I looked through my list, it quickly became apparent that the items listed were robbing me of my time with those three most important aspects. What was I thinking in letting so many events and commitments dominate my life?

On Friday, the first item taken to the dumpster was the run for senate. I had been warned prior to running that this would take precious time away from the family, stretch my faith, and take a lot of money. Also, I could not afford to strain relationships in our community where I sought to be a light to others. My opponent lived only three streets over, was a friend of mine, and had a good reputation. He was just simply was an attorney in the wrong party. Those two reasons alone are what compelled me to run, but was it worth it? The answer was no.

This decision meant calling the gentleman I had chosen to head my campaign to alert him of my departure from the campaign. I called Senator Jim DeMint's Chief of Staff, Brett Bernhardt and Senator Lindsay Graham's Chief, Richard Perry. I also made a call directly to Congressman Joe Wilson to let him know of my decision, as he had heard of my tumor. Though each one had personally vowed to help me in my run and each shared their willingness to support my endeavors, they were all in agreement with my decision and sent me well wishes for a speedy recovery.

Saturday came around and, after some morning time with the family, I began to run up and down the list of board positions. I was immediately able to discern which ones would benefit from me leaving their boards. Did you get that? Which ones would benefit from me leaving them? They didn't need me. Then, I went through and struck through the names of those boards that I had no passion about their mission or what they did. One by one, I struck every single one of them off but one. I didn't strike off one board position because I thought I could be an influencer on this board for both business and politics. It would take me three years before I would realize that I was fooling myself.

The next Sunday, as was custom, the morning involved getting everyone fed, dressed, and off to church. When we arrived at church, it was apparent that everyone knew about my cancer diagnosis. The hugs, kisses, and encouraging statements were a great pick-me-up. It is great to have the support and love of friends in our life.

It was during the service that I came to the realization that serving on the diaconate was not where I needed to be either. I needed to finish my duties, but if asked, I did not need to serve the next time around. I really did not enjoy being in meetings where decisions couldn't be made without moving through several committees. When the nominating committee approached me about coming back on the diaconate, I said, "No, thank you." It was not significant to me any longer. Not knowing what was ahead of me, the decision was to spend more time with young men, mentoring them in the areas of marriage, business, and the deepening of their faith. Our church is one of the biggest and most influential churches in Columbia. Being recognized by the leaders as a possible leader in the church is a tremendous honor. However, in the same way that a prominent, non-profit board position feeds our desire for status, a church position can have the same enticement. Not that I came on for that reason, but it is easy to get drawn into that frame of mind that your importance is measured in your position in the church. This is absolutely not true. It can become junk in your life.

On Monday morning, I sent my assistant a text to let her know that I would not be in that day. I needed to complete the spring-cleaning of my life. I had not finished "sweeping out" many of the areas of my life that needed thorough cleaning.

We had started the software firm in the spring of 2001. It was now five years later, almost exactly to the date when I told our board I would commit to five years of running Acadia. My goal was to start it, sell it, cash-out, and start another. I had become a serial entrepreneur, but not intentionally. I found a passion for starting companies. With this, I determined that I would work diligently to sell Acadia and keep my consulting and services firm called Root Loud, my real passion in business. I informed Marion, my largest investor and mentor, that I was going to be intentional about getting Acadia ready for sale. Now I had it. I would scratch the following off:

- Run for state senate
- All board positions and committees
- Diaconate at church
- Sell Acadia, one of my software companies
- Say no to all requests for boards and committees for a at least three years

After checking off these insignificant items, I now had time to focus on the most significant things in my life. Think of how much time I would now be able to devote to my faith, my wife, and my children. The amount of time I could devote to top priority items enabled me to set a clear direction for the rest of that year.

As I look back, I ask myself, "What was I thinking?" I had bought into the American businessman's "value system." In business, you are taught that you are to be involved in the community and join numerous boards or organizations. It was simply the way you were supposed to influence and gain influence, no matter the personal costs.

A friend in Florida, who rose to become one of the top bankers in the country, told me on a recent weekend getaway that he had looked back at his schedule during the height of his career and found that he was spending the majority of his time in business meetings and after-hours dinners; plus, a large portion of his time, which should have been family time, was spent at fundraisers and community events. He didn't realize how much time had been robbed from his life until he semi-retired after the acquisition of his bank. It was at that time that he committed himself to serving the bank and never took another full-time position. He was fortunate to have been successful early in his career so that if afforded him the ability to be with his children and wife.

Recently, my friend completed over five hundred miles of

hiking the Appalachian Trail with two daughters. His simplified life also gave him the freedom to spend time skiing, visiting colleges, and traveling with his eighteen-year-old son prior to his departure for college. My friend was fortunate. He became aware of the traps we businessmen fall into and had the time and resources to right his ship before it collided with a rocky shore.

Is the need to entertain just a part of doing business or is it too an unnecessary activity in our life? If we can't build a relationship during work hours, does buying dinners or golf outings give us the opportunity to bond with our business prospects? Is the time we spend entertaining our prospects more worthwhile than entertaining our children or our spouses? We ignore the lasting legacy in making memories with our family, and work our butts off for a legacy of making a name in business and community.

Louis Upkins, author of *Treat Me Like a Customer*, has written a great book that gives us insight to treating our spouses like we do our customers. Just think what our families would look like if we did give the same attention and customer service to our families as we do our customers. Upkins' simple, commonsense approach to improving our work-life balance is what most business, church, and non-profit managers need when they see imbalance in their lives.

Some questions to ask yourself

When I used to plant watermelons, if I did not remove the weeds around the vine, the weeds would choke the vine and rob me of watermelons. Are you removing the weeds in your life? If so, what are they? (Humorous note: Don't insert your spouse, mother-in-law, or children here.)

What will it take for you to begin prioritizing your life? What will be first, second, and third on your list?

If you asked your spouse or children what they desire most to do with you, would you be willing to arrange your schedule and do it?

Chapter 13

The Real Cost of Junk in our Lives

No one can accurately determine the cost of junk in our lives. How do we measure lost opportunities? How do we see days wasting away due to the mental and physical stress on our bodies? So what does junk in your life really cost you? It is something we all have to weigh, figuratively and literally. As a good friend of mine says, decisions, good or bad, have costs and consequences. Let's try and evaluate the cost and consequences of junk in our lives. Let's prioritize our life according to our passions, goals, and vision for the future. The freedom and blessing we gain, in the end, will all be worth it.

If we start from the very beginning looking at what a storage-unit costs, this will give us some indication as to the actual cost of acquiring and hoarding, whether significant or insignificant. Let's begin with an elderly woman who has stored her items at my friend's self-storage unit for more than ten years. She has paid an average of $50 a month for ten years. That equates to $600 per year, or $6,000 since moving her junk in. When I asked my friend what he felt he could get for the things in her unit if she were to walk away and leave him holding next month's bill, he replied, "very little." Now remember, she has paid over $6,000, and he doesn't even think he could get $300 for her items if she stopped payment today.

We know the current and past cost of her items, so now let's look at the opportunity she missed out on. Remember, we must look not only at today's impact on junk in our lives but the opportunities it erases. If she had invested the $600 for the last 10 years at a 10% return, she would now have $12,000 in the bank. To her it may not matter, but to her children or even grandchildren, that amount would pay for at least one year of college, if not two. I will bet if you asked her today whether she would like to gift her granddaughter $12,000 for her college education or give $6,000 to store her items that don't fit in her home, she would say she'd rather help her granddaughter. We don't think about tomorrow, we think only about now, and I am as guilty of this as anyone.

Do you remember the words of the owner of the self-storage facility in that tiny small town when I asked him what was in those units? Many times, even his customers forget what is in their units. They also "forget" to pay him for renting those units. Ultimately, they know they are paying to store junk. What many eventually decide is that making the payment on the bass boat, season tickets, or a golf vacation is far more important than paying for the storage of their junk. He might say, "What would happen if I lost my storage unit? Nothing is in there anyway." We do attribute value to pretty much everything in our lives, but we never put it down on a checklist and prioritize.

My friend has a contract agreement with each renter of his storage-units. If you fail to pay your fees after a certain period of time, he is able to sell everything in your unit in order to recoup the money you owe him. As you can imagine, this is a tremendous hassle for him. He'd much rather you just pay him.

The law gives a lot of protection to the renter, so he has to notify the person many times that they are late, and get legal authority to approve the fact they are in default. Then, he must run ads in the local paper of the upcoming auction of the unit's items with a brief overview of what is coming up for auction. Again, he'd much prefer the renters pay their $50 per month bill.

When he goes through all of this hassle and has the auction, he is selling significant, expensive items and simply getting his money back right? Wrong! In ten years and more than fifteen auctions, he has only recovered the fees owed to him one time. Did you get that? He has only recovered what was owed to him one time since owning his self-storage units.

For example, if someone owed him for six months rent, that would be $300 (6 months x $50 per month). So if he sold the items in that self-storage unit, he would need to collect $300 to get his money back, not counting the time, cost, and hassle for setting up the auction. Even in his agreements, if he collects what is owed him, he has to mail the renter a check for the difference.

I laugh thinking about the poor soul who gets a notice that his things are being auctioned for non-payment. Here he is going to the mailbox everyday, knowing they are going to get money for their items above what is owed to my friend. This person thought that their items were significant and valuable. They wait and wait for the check, but it never arrives. Only in time do they realize that what they had in their unit was mere junk.

We fail to think about the cost of looking for a treasure at garage sales and flea markets. The people who do this do it religiously. Their dream is to end up on the *Antique Roadshow* with their big find. A typical scenario might involve an older gentleman who claims he is a garage sale junkie. He stands before an antiquities dealer for the *Antique Roadshow* to share his recent garage sale find. Knowing he might have something rare, since he was one of eight chosen for the show, he beams with excitement. The dealer points out the intricate details of his item, hinting it may be rare. How much could it be worth? As the expert conveys his obvious knowledge of this era of art, the viewers anxiously wait for the estimate to be revealed. The big moment comes with the dealer saying the piece could bring $500 to $700 at auction. The elder man had accomplished something that none of his garage sale friends had yet to accomplish. He had turned a five-dollar buy into $500. The question is, had he? Regretfully, we look at the value of this piece of history and fail to remember the hours, the days, and the weeks wasted away looking for a $500 piece of treasure. Inevitably, this item will be sold at the garage sale his son holds after his father dies.

If you read the book, *Same Kind of Different as Me*, you may remember the conversation over a cup of coffee where the home-less man, Denver, asks the rich guy, Ron, about all the keys on his key chain. "Mr. Ron," he asks, "Do you own them or do they own you?" From what I have seen in the lives of those around me, and even in my own life, we allow these things to own us. The more we make, the bigger the toys we acquire. Each one has its own key. It includes property at the beach, the farm in the country, the condo for the home football games, and the Suburban we need to haul all our belongings.

So, ask yourself this question. What can I give away or sell at my next garage sale? Not only did our family donate the unsold things from our yard sale to local ministries, we donated a portion of our cash as well. It wasn't much, but it had made an impact.

To get a good idea of what your junk is costing you, give a call to 800-Got-Junk and let them come to your home or business and give you a free quote. It won't cost you a dime for the quote, but it will reveal the cost of keeping insignificant things around your home. If you don't mind the clutter or inability to move freely through your home, garage, or attic, then just let it keep accumulat-ing. Don't worry; your children will inevitably have to deal with it when the time comes.

Ask your spouse what habits you have that need to be thrown out to the curb for hauling off. Ask your children what they want to do? Be strong enough to recognize it, strong enough to apologize for it, and strong enough to ask for accountability in staying the course.

Here are two things that are simple to do. Go get your online bank statement, your credit card statement, and calendar and lay them before you on paper. Start with your bank statement and credit card statement. Highlight in yellow those things that are must haves. These should be the "highlight" of your life. In red, mark the junk in your life that you don't need and is causing pain or stress in your life. Use a green marker to see those items you have invested in and could potentially invest more when the red is gone. It could be your retirement, family vacation, kid's college, tithing to your church, and so on. All other items not marked simply need to be given priority in your life.

For your calendar, this is just as hard. Again, with the yellow marker, mark those items that are the highlight of your week or month. I hope you can find dates with your spouse and time with the family on a long-weekend getaway. Next, get out that red marker and begin striking through those events that are not significant in your life and the life of your family. Be deliberate. In green, mark those items where you are investing in relationships that matter. It should be focused around the investments you make that include mentoring, Bible study, and accountability. Be careful not to let four nights of your son's baseball game get marked in yellow or green. The family, not junior, needs to agree on where these activities fall within the life of the family.

In the last two years, we instituted 8:30 p.m. as Mommy/Daddy Time for the rest of the evening. Ashley and I go to bed around ten o'clock, so that gave us approximately an hour and a half to unwind, relax, and talk. Several years back, Ashley and I started having a date night at least twice a month. Many times, we do get four dates in during the month. Why? If we don't specifically set our lives apart from our children, our lives will mirror their lives instead of their lives mirroring our lives. The key here is that your children are an appendage to you. The most important thing fathers and mothers can do for their children is to love one another and be unabashedly selfish about time with each other. Men, this isn't watching the Thursday night game of the week. Ladies, this isn't about reading the latest gossip magazine. This is about conversation and intimacy with each other. If you have this, not only will your marriages be stronger, your children will bring less junk into their own marriages later on.

So what is preventing you from cleaning out? Is there fear that you'll get rid of something important? Is there a concern that it will take too long? Remember, in my story, it took a mere four days to get my priorities in line and to mark off the junk I did not need.

What is preventing you from growing in your job or growing your company? Don't begin with your "need" to get another degree, or a "need" to work more hours each week. I have heard this too many times in my sixteen years of business. Look closely at what areas of junk you can remove from your daily grind and spend that time on becoming better and more proficient in your current job. Look at your schedule and make time for your purpose and calling. Read purposeful books and periodicals to give you insight and enable you to achieve success, not mediocrity.

We look at the neighbor's double-car garage stuffed with boxes, old dining room rugs, and a myriad of other items with no significant value. While the cost may not appear as great as the lady's $50 a month storage bill, it still puts your new car in the direct hit of nature, scooters, and baseballs. Ultimately, the unused items in your garage could be of benefit to a child or family. In your garage is merely cluttering for your life.

I think back to when Ashley and I moved into our first home. It took a small U-Haul truck to come to my apartment to get my things, and simply one more trip to get Ashley's things at her apartment. In two short trips with a small truck, our move was complete. Not long after we were married, we acquired the normal furniture for our new home. Then it was a new dining room table, and before long, the house was full. At this point in our lives, we did not have a garage, had nothing in the attic, and nothing under the house.

Two years later, we moved to our current home. On the day we moved, I distinctly remember boxing up certain items at our old home and taking them straight to the attic of our new home.

When I went into the attic a few weeks back for our big garage sale, that same exact box with the same tape was sitting virtually in the same place I had put it thirteen years ago. While it was my wife's family items that I am not at liberty to remove, it still sits there today. To me, it is insignificant, but to her, grandmother's china is significant. It is just not significant enough to make it to our china cabinet. Why? Our china cabinet is full of our wedding china that hasn't been used in three years.

Still, thanks to our garage sale, the garage is easy to move through and the attic is seemingly empty, except for our Christmas ornaments. The kitchen drawers have room again. The cabinets aren't full of old crystal, candleholders, and never used pots.

Recently, one area of cleaning out was at my office. I was paying more $2,000 a month in rent and utilities. I travel quite a bit so the office was more for our Root Loud team than it was for me. When I came to realize that half my staff had young children at home, and they were responding to my questions and client needs via email into late in the night, it occurred to me that they should just work from home. Surely it would be easier for them to balance their work and family schedule from home. I have come to find that we are more productive working from home, and our employees can attend to their children's needs with less interference.

This move not only saved me money, it removed those items costing me money. Those items, seeming to be significant, really were not significant at all. Most of our clients are in other cites around the country, so the office was created to facilitate client visits. Working from home also freed me from having to manage people daily, which clearly wasn't needed with the team I now had. It allowed me to focus on our company's strengths and slough off those areas that were burdens. We are now much more focused and flexible in meeting our clients' needs.

Think about how many hours a typical family spends away from each other in a day. Pile on activities like soccer, baseball, ballet, and homework. I have read studies stating that family time together is about fifty minutes a day, a mere 3 percent of your total minutes in the day. By working from home, and when not traveling, I now get to eat and interact with my family the entire day. It is truly a blessing I had not realized.

Some questions to ask yourself

Calculate the real cost (not value) of junk in your life. Now weigh it against the value of your life.

Go back to page 100. Pull out your last bank statement and your calendar. Anything strike you or signal your priorities in life?

Do you really know how valuable you are? I recommend you read Romans 8:35-39 and John 3:16. Who was Jesus speaking to in John 3:16? What was his position? (see verse John 3:1 for the answer)

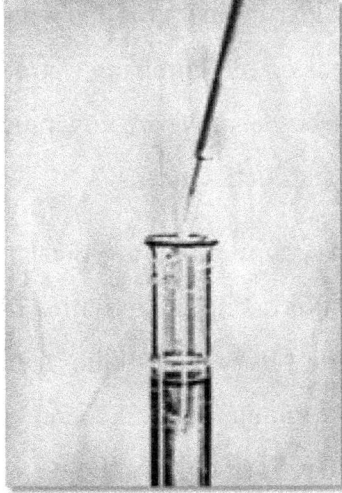

Chapter 14

The Lab Results

It had been five days since my colonoscopy revealed the tumor in my colon. It was now Tuesday, the day I was to hear the biopsy results. I remember getting up and having a sense of freedom. Amazingly, I was not anxious about hearing the results but, of course, I did want the answer. It is amazing that when you put your focus on your real purpose in life, and nothing else, you can have peace even in times of uncertainty.

It was in the afternoon when I got the call from the doctor's office. My heart skipped a beat when I answered to find out it was the doctor's office. The nurse immediately said she had good news. The tumor was benign. Amazing relief swept over me. I would not have to go through hours of additional tests, treatments, or medicines. The immediate plan was to get surgery scheduled to remove the tumor, a portion of the colon, and my appendix.

Within a few weeks of that call, I would be wheeled out of the hospital with the physical junk removed, as well as all the other junk in my life. Untethered to a tumor and unnecessary commitments in my life, I could now live freely and passionately for those things that were most important. I was told to go home and rest for two weeks. With my new schedule, I could easily handle that without any worrying. Yet, it would take three years to truly eradicate all the items I vowed to strike off my personal junk list.

In September of 2009, more than three years later, the Chairman of the Board at Acadia and I signed the papers for the sale of the software company. Now I only had one company, and that was Root Loud. Soon after selling Acadia, I resigned from my very last board position. I had completely achieved the freedom I desired. The pure blessing came in time spent with family, my men's accountability group, date nights, mentoring, and sharing with friends in need.

Just before I sold the company in September 2009, I was on a plane flight late on a Friday afternoon. An exhausted, sixty yea old man plopped down beside me. The long exhale told the story. We began to share tidbits about our lives. It was apparent that he loved his work and his family. When I shared the young ages of my children, he smiled as if to say, "I miss those days."

In our sharing, he talked about his hectic schedule due to business commitments and outside board positions. I shared with him the fact that I had made a decision to remove all that from my life so that I could focus on those things significant in my life. He was shocked when I had mentioned that I owned a company, yet did not serve on boards or committees in the community. I shared how a small tumor changed my life and my life's priorities.

As we were wrapping up the discussion and the details, which he inquired about, he said, "I am fifty-nine and I wish God had allowed me to have a tumor at thirty-nine." He went on to tell me that he had recently realized, with his last child leaving home, that all the board meetings, social events, and client dinners had robbed him of time with the most precious gifts he had. He had realized that those things most significant in his life had been treated more like junk. We all come to ask ourselves these questions at some point in our lives. Regretfully for most, it comes too late to correct it. As the late Mark Twain said, "Death focuses the mind wonderfully." Don't allow any more time to slip away. Live a life without any more regrets.

Some questions to ask yourself

When you are 59 and thinking about the time you spent (or could have spent) with your family, will you be happy or look back with disappointment?

At the next funeral service you attend, listen intently on what is said of the person. Did kind of legacy did that person leave?

"Death focuses the mind wonderfully." - Mark Twain

Chapter 15

No Junk! Well Much Less of It

How can we avoid some of life's pitfalls and follow the road to living life to its fullest? I must warn you, it is a narrow way and not many people are on it. In some cases we need hedges or even guardrails. Hedges prevent us from seeing the Jones' things. These might include a bigger home, a second home, a new boat, or a nice convertible. Hedges act as blinders for our eyes, much like those worn y the horses you see pulling the carriages in downtown Charleston. They help us avoid distractions and stay focused on the proper reference points. I am a person who has to use blinders in life. I am the compulsive buyer. If I need it, I buy it. The only thing I do well is to get rid of it when I don't use it any longer. I have wasted more money that I care to admit due to impulsive buying. Thanks to putting myself on a budget this year, my buying behavior is improved.

The other item we need in life is guardrails. Think about the guardrails on the road. They are purposely positioned in places of danger or areas where we could hurt ourselves. They don't sit in our path of travel, but just off the path. They also aren't placed where the danger is. No, they are situated in between where we need to be and where we don't need to be. We still have room to move, make minor adjustments, and be protected from dangers.

Just like the guardrails on our interstates or mountain roads, we need guardrails in our lives. For me, I need them in my finances and in my desire for other things. I call it "man disease." I have two great friends who help me here. In my finances, my wife is the accountability partner. She is a coupon shopper and knows how to save money. Fifteen years of marriage, coupled with my bad spending habits, have had their effects on her. She is not as tight as she was when we got married (even though I wish she were). Having one checking account is a great tool for couples, like us, with different spending habits. Checking accounts are not like his and her towels in a bathroom, where you have one and she has one.

What hedges do you need to plant and what guardrails do you need to install? Also, who will help you keep the hedges healthy and the guardrails repaired. Trust me, you'll attempt to trim the hedges way low so you can see more of what your neighbors have acquired. You will also have some minor scrapes from rubbing against those guardrails. You will probably even knock a few down. When you do, have a friend there to help you repair and cement them in the ground even more than before. Once you see that you can bust through, you will try even harder. Remember, you are overcoming an addiction. You have to admit it and get help. It is the small things that creep in, grow bigger and bigger. It could be cancer, pornography, lust, or money. It will creep up on you and destroy you, your marriage, and your family if you are not careful.

About four years ago, shortly after the medical awakening, I heard a friend talking about camping. My friend is not what you'd call an outdoorsman. While I am no Grizzly Adams, I do hunt, surf, fish, sail, and hike. My buddy was telling me about how much his family liked to go camping. Now, let me make it clear upfront that we are not talking about tent camping. This is RV camping or travel trailer camping.

My wife prefers flip-flops, a good pair of comfortable shorts, and a comfortable t-shirt, just like I do. My kids would wear bathing suits and go barefoot all year long if we'd allow it. We are a very laid back family who really like to be comfortable.

Most wives don't enjoy the outdoors like my wife. Ashley and I spent our honeymoon hiking the Grand Tetons in Wyoming, whitewater rafting, fly-fishing, and horseback riding in Big Sky. On our first anniversary, we scaled 1,000-plus feet up the side of a mountain on the Precipice Trail, the most challenging hiking trail in Acadia National Park in Maine.

My kids love climbing, hiking, fishing, and campfires. They love the outdoors. We were made for camping. We acquired our first camper shortly after my tumor was removed. After four years of camping, we still find it hard to go home from our trips. Even our friends now join us in camping adventures.

So what does camping have to do with junk? That is a very simple answer. When you camp, even in our 30-foot travel trailer, you realize that all the things back at your 3,800 square foot home don't bring the joys of life that you think they do. The camper basically has bunk beds, queen bed, a kitchen, a dining area, and a couch. All of this fits amazingly within about 270 square feet – one-tenth the size of our home. We are so close together, unencumbered by walls and distance, that we bond as a family like no other time.

At home, we have 3,800 square feet more of space than our camper in order to get away from each other. What I have realized is that the closer we are together as a family, the closer we really get with each other emotionally. It seems it would be the opposite, but it is not. We are the most content with each other while camping.

For our kids, camping means leaving scooters, swing set, trampoline, and friends. What it provides them is an outlet for their God-given creativity and imagination. Sticks become swords, canopy trees become forts, and the freedom of the campground is equal to the 200-acre property I grew up on. Camping to my kids is like a C. S. Lewis book being recreated in reality.

For Ashley and me, it is a sweet reunion every time. Being together as a family brings so much joy. We camp approximately six times a year for a total of twenty-five days in a year. We find we only need things of significance that include each other, food and clothes.

As in our garages, attics and self-storage units, the clutter hides or even dims the brightness of those things most significant. When the clutter is removed, the important things shine. They regain their importance and begin to fulfill the needs we have in life. As you can see, camping is a spiritual house-cleaning activity for us.

When we go, we are removed from the items that separate us, and prevent us, from the sweet time together. Camping is a reminder to us of what is important. It is just evidence that our kids internally desire it as well.

If you and your family want to shed the junk from around your family, go rent a state park cabin, which usually is lacking in amenities such as a television. The most important thing is to be far enough away that your cell phone won't work. I can promise you that your kids will appreciate your cell not working and the fact that you aren't checking emails every minute. For the kids, be sure to leave the Nintendo DS's and iPods at home. Let them hear nature sing, not Taylor Swift or Lady Gaga.

A close friend's father has been a success at virtually everything he has ever done. In high school, college, and in business, he had the ability to accomplish goals many of us merely dreamed of. In the years I was around him the most, his demeanor intimidated me. He is an impressive, stately man and known throughout Charleston for his business and political success. He loved his wife, kids, and grandchildren dearly. He was a man's man by all accounts.

I came to see he was a real man a few years ago when he quit everything in order to stay at home and be beside his ailing wife. A beauty queen, state tennis champ, and mother to four amazing children was stricken with Alzheimer's. Seeing him become a servant to the lady that had served him many years was one of the most beautiful sights anyone could behold. Those years of taking care of every need showed me more about this man than all the business and political accomplishments he ever achieved. It was in that time that he showed me how to be a man.

There will be fear in taking steps to removing the clutter in your life. In the movie *Braveheart*, we see William Wallace on the line with his troops prior to battle. While he is able to detect the fear in the eyes of his men, what he sees most is the freedom he and his countrymen can gain from winning this epic battle. His words to his men are words we can all take to heart.

"And dying in your beds, many years from now, would you be willing to trade ALL the days, from this day to that, for one chance, just one chance, to come back here and tell our enemies that they may take our lives, but they'll never take... OUR FREEDOM!"

William Wallace knew that freedom took sacrifice. I am not here to say that the freedom you'll gain in removing the junk in your life is of the same epic proportions as being on the battle line. What I am saying is that moving toward freedom, much like that of Wallace's men, requires you to move forward in confidence. You don't want to be dying in your bed wishing for that one last chance to make a difference in your life and the lives of those around you. Whether it is your home, body, mind, family, business, or church, taking the first step to changing your behavior could impact life and eternity. Our enemy stands before us in the mirror each day. You can see the enemy, and you can change the enemy. It will require help and accountability.

Thankfully, we are blessed with those around us to help us in this battle. Your neighbor, sister, pastor, psychologist, or doctor can stand beside you as you move forward to achieve freedom and a clear direction. Trust me when I say that it is impossible to explain what is gained by shedding the things that weigh us down. Our ability to move freely in life, living with fewer encumbrances, is what we should desire. Don't continue to weigh yourself down with junk, debt, mental clutter, physical issues, or past events. Don't buy into the American Dream, if it means becoming overwhelmed with insignificant "stuff." Look closely at this lie and see the slave it makes of us. No one wants to be a slave, but we allow the world to put its shackles on us in so many ways.

Recently I had the opportunity to spend two days with ten wealthy businessmen. Many of my close friends who knew of this trip wanted to know what we had talked about. Did they talk about money? Did they give great insight to their investments? The answer is: They did talk about money and their investments, but not in the way that you are probably thinking. These men were absolutely deliberate and obedient with every penny. These men, as well as their children and grandchildren, had clear objectives in their spending and in their giving. They had accountability, those hedges and guardrails, in their own personal life. They had more plans for giving their resources away than they had for spending them. I am talking cash money, buildings, time, and their most precious item, their faith. These men lived out their faith like none I had ever seen. They were truly servant leaders, and they were generous givers.

If you ever want to experience this for yourself, drive on the campus of Berry College in Rome, Georgia. This college is beautifully landscaped, and it is the largest college, in land mass, in the world. What is most wonderful about this campus is that it also is the home of the WinShape Foundation Headquarters. Established by Chick-fil-A founder Truett Cathy, WinShape boasts many buildings, homes, and ministries that include orphanages, youth camps, wilderness adventure camps, marriage retreats, and an international ministry that reaches the entire globe. Truett could have merely spent the millions he invested in these ministries to children and families. The "chicken sandwich" has allowed Truett, his wife, children, and grandchildren to invest in the lives of those who are broken or in need. Instead of acquiring items that would become rust and dust, the Truetts have chosen to invest in those things that last an eternity. The old saying is so true! "Don't judge the day by the harvest you reap, but by the seeds you sow."

Today, life for my family and me is so much simpler. There are no board meetings, there is only one company to run, and dinner most every night is spent together as family. I enjoy sitting on my daughter's bed helping her write music, making paper airplanes with my son, and chasing another daughter around the home for a good tickle. My relationship with my wife is so much stronger. I still have my usual tendencies that cause her to roll her eyes. Yet, our love for each other is so much more than it was sixteen years ago. Our walks, date nights, and camping continue to strengthen our relationship. Last, and most importantly, I now find the time I need for prayer and the study of scripture. My relationship with my Creator is now a more intimate relationship. It is a work in progress, but it is progress.

My only request is that you make time and get to know the God who made you so wonderfully. While we all have changes to make in our life, the only thing He requires of you is to come as you are. Trust me, He wants you where you are and as you are. As He did me, He will provide answers and make the necessary changes in your life when He is ready. For me, it was at the age of thirty-nine, but for the man on the plane, it was fifty-nine. What He can provide, the American Dream cannot. His dream for you is so much more that any of us can ever imagine.

I hope you can find peace, clarity, and freedom as you move

toward getting rid of the junk in your life. I pray that your relationships grow closer and sweeter. May you find time to sow, not reap, love in those around you, leaving a legacy for eternity.

As Dr. Billy Graham said, "The legacy we leave is not just our possessions, but in the quality of our lives. What preparations should we be making now? The greatest waste in all the earth, which cannot be recycled or reclaimed, is our waste of the time that God has given us each day."

Some questions to ask yourself

What guardrails do you need to put in place for your life? What do you need to be protected from?

What hedges to you need to put in place for you life? What do you not need to see?

Go to www.guardrailsandhedges.com to get insights on staying focused on life.

Are you willing to work hard to save your family or had you rather save your reputation? What means more to you?

Chapter 16

Bent Reality

Dr. Wendell Estep, the pastor at First Baptist Church in Columbia, South Carolina, told me a story about growing up in East Texas. It was here, while Dr. Estep was in his youth, that a new boy moved into town. One day, Wendell's inquisitive new friend asked him this question. "Why do the trees in east Texas point north?" Being completely puzzled, Wendell replied that their trees don't point to the north. So the young man told Wendell to come outside and see. When Wendell got his bearings right as to which direction north was, he found that his friend wasn't kidding. The trees really did point to the north. The reason was fairly simple. There is a consistent northerly movement of wind off the Gulf of Mexico that pushes the trees to the north, whereby they grow leaning north.

Our lives today closely mimic that of the East Texas trees. We are constantly being pushed by the winds of change so much that we fail to realize the bending of our values. Our values and direction become as warped as the trees in East Texas. The winds of our society will not cease to blow and pressure our lives and families; however, we can begin to lay foundations that will keep us on solid ground. We need to make a stand and plant ourselves firmly against the winds of change. This process first starts with us, individually. Then, it moves through our families, our neighborhoods, cities, and beyond.

Marriage is one of those areas where the pushing of the incessant winds has affected the family. The November 18, 2010, Associated Press article, "Is Marriage Going Away," reports that recent surveys show thirty-nine percent of Americans said "marriage was becoming obsolete." Confirming this trend is the recent Census Bureau report that opposite-sex unmarried couples living together jumped thirteen percent to a whopping 7.5 million. As a society, we have an inability to make and keep long-term commitments. Confirming this statement is the fact that 29 percent of children under the age of eighteen now live with a parent or parents who are unwed or no longer married.

An area we need to correct, after we correct ourselves, involves our children and the notion that we are all to be equal, no matter what. We have allowed society (including politicians and the court system) to tell us that we should all be exactly the same. We are not. Here are some areas of my life that are most likely distinct from many of you reading this book:

1. I was put up for adoption at birth and adopted at five weeks old.
2. I was adopted by a lower-middle class paper mill mechanic, not an actor or pop star.
3. My job during high school involved raising watermelons and plowing family farms.

You get the picture. I am not complaining, but it sure would have been nice when I launched my first company in 1995 to have been given the money by my father. Instead, I had to borrow

$100,000 in my own name in order to kick-start the company. Here are some examples of how we have allowed this notion of "all being equal" to enter our lives and the lives of our children. These are some example of the mediocrity we are encouraging in our children:

- We don't keep scores at little league games because "everyone" is a winner.
- We don't give trophies to the "best student" or "best athlete" any longer; we give them to everybody on the team.
- We don't give scores under a "C" in our classes in school.
- We teach to the lowest achiever in class, while our achievers are pulled down.

We are not all created equal, thankfully. We are all created uniquely. We should treat others, no matter how high or low in society they may be viewed, as we desire to be treated. However, we cannot get around the fact we are different and that is what makes life so amazing and wonderful. We have different gifts, different needs, and different perspectives. Each one of us makes up a beautifully designed puzzle.

As I speak around the country on the topic of removing the junk in our lives and experiencing life as it was meant to be, I hear story after story as to the devastation this junk imposes on our families. Men, women, couples, successful businessmen, and pastors all point to the fact that they have climbed the ladder of success, only to realize the ladder was on the wrong wall. Once you realize that you have been swallowed whole by this so-called "American Dream," you may beat your head upon the mirror asking yourself this question: "What have I done?"

If I may, I'd like to offer you this advice. If you have made it through this book and are asking yourself this same question, please know that you have just taken a huge step. I find (notice the present tense of the verb find) myself praying to God, asking Him to intervene and get me out of the many predicaments that I seem to put myself in. While you may take a different approach at first, you will find that over time, this crisis we are so concerned with will pass. It will become a mere story to others in the future. How you respond, and how you navigate at that moment, ultimately shapes who and where you will be tomorrow. Don't take the decision lightly, as it has mighty consequences. As with my colon tumor, no matter how bad it may have seemed at the time, today it is simply my story. It is now a story about a thirty-nine year-old fella' who changed his direction in order to be the man his wife desired, the father his children spend time with, and the friend to others in time of need. Your predicament will become your story. What will it be?

How we move, after realizing our state of mind and behavior, is critical. For people like Dave Ramsey, he did a 180 degree turn and went in the opposite direction. However, not all of us have this will. Just making a few adjustments in a positive direction is a good sign. In sailing, you never hold the helm in a constant position. The wind, waves, and currents move your boat constantly. With that shifting motion, you are required to adjust over and over.

I want to leave you with one last story. Remember I mentioned my first wedding anniversary trip to Bar Harbor? I told you about the awesome climb up Precipice Mountain. What I failed to mention may be the most important part of the story. The climb up the mountain was exhilarating and beautiful. However, when we reached the top of the mountain, there were warning signs not to climb back down the mountain but to take a trail down the backside. We did as warned and began meandering around this trail. It was hard to follow this trail, as it is not as traveled as one might think. When we climbed the mountain that day, we only ran into four couples. As we moved down the backside, we had to look closely for where others had walked before. Thankfully, someone had stacked rocks into the shape of a pyramid, called cairns, to mark where the trailed turned. The walk down was not an issue. The issue was staying on the trail.

When we finally reached the bottom of the mountain, I turned around. Amazingly, from the bottom of the trail looking up, you could clearly see the trail from the top down. From my new perspective, I could now see the path cut between the brush and hills. Isn't that a lot like life? As we move, each step is taken with some hesitation. We ask ourselves, "Is this the right way?" Ultimately, when we get to a certain point and look back, we are amazed at how it all turned out.

Each night when we pray with our kids, I pray: "Father, I want to thank you for the ways we have seen You protect us today. We really thank You for those unseen times when you directed and protected us from our bad decisions and from others' bad decisions." Think about the times when you went against your instincts or that voice telling you not to go there. I know that when I find myself in a situation I don't like, I sometimes ignore that warning voice. After so many mistakes, I am more inclined to listen to that voice, and to my wife, who often seems to echo that same voice.

One last point I'd like to make is this: If you think that you have gone so far that you can't get back up, let me encourage you in this: it is never too late. First, you have to surrender to your selfish, deceitful desires. Second, you need to find a person(s) who you can go to in confidence and share that area of need in your life. If your issue is serious, I will suggest these three should be welcomed into your life:

- Faith to recognize you are a great creation in the hands of a mighty Creator.
- A counselor or psychologist who is an expert in

the area of your need.

- A close friend(s) to walk with you and care deeply about you.

Remember, in life we need hedges and guardrails in every area. We may act like we have this life all figured out, but we know we don't. We are simply a constant work in progress. Life is hard. Our society punishes us if we don't conform to it.

Let me give you a firsthand testimony about life.

"No", I won't join that board."

"No, I won't let my son play baseball on Sundays."

"No, I won't let pornography destroy my family and me."

"No, I won't buy on credit, because I don't have the money."

"No, I won't sit and watch television tonight, I am going on a walk with my wife."

The more you say NO, the easier life is to live and to enjoy. Today, I have more freedom to move, more clarity to see, and more time to spend, because of a tumor at the age of thirty-nine.

Today, I can truly say that I am experiencing life as God meant for it to be experienced. There are still times of difficulty and times of pain, but these tough times are outweighed by the joy and peace I now how. My hope is that you too will find that same joy and peace in life.

Some questions to ask yourself

As in the story of the bent trees in East Texas, what bent reality has become real to you?

What impact has culture, or even your neighbors, had on your way of living?

Look in the mirror tonight and practice saying "NO." It may allow you to live a life with less regrets. It did for me.

In Luke 15, how many friends do you think the prodigal son had before he squandered his wealth? How many did he have after all his wealth was lost?

People who really care about you don't care where you live, what you drive, or where you work. They care about you.

THE END

About the Author

Mitch Smith, at the age of twenty-seven, founded his first interactive, technology firm and went on to launch four additional technology companies. These web-based software firms focused on learning management, performance appraisals, and applicant tracking. In his seventeen years of business, Mitch's greatest joy has been serving as founder and CEO of Root Loud (rootloud. com), an education-based sales and people development firm based in Columbia, South Carolina. In his career, Mitch has been responsible for creating processes and software that run some of the world's largest corporate universities. These include: Aflac, Biovail Pharmaceuticals, Bose, Dow Chemical, Hewlett Packard, Red Lobster, Nike, Nokia, and Southeastern Freight Lines. He has worked with over 280 corporations around the world.

Since his tumor in 2005, Mitch continues to abstain from service on any boards. He enjoys the outdoors with his family, and his hobbies include camping, sailing, hunting, and fly-fishing. Mitch has been married to Ashley, his wife for, over sixteen years. They have been blessed with three children: Erin, Boyd, and Mary Claire.

Mitch is a 1990 graduate of The Citadel and served seven years in the South Carolina Army National Guard. He completed a one-year study of Christian worldview under Chuck Colson in the Centurions Program.

Follow Mitch!

www.mitchdsmith.com

Twitter:

https://twitter.com/mitchdsmith

Facebook:

http://www.facebook.com/mitchsmithfb

Linkedin:

http://www.linkedin.com/in/mitchsmith

Bring Mitch D. Smith to your organization!

Mitch D. Smith is internationally known for strategic planning/ direction and education-based initiatives. His sixteen years of work for corporations and non-profits which include Aflac, Darden Restaurants, Dow Chemical, Hewlett-Packard, Nokia, Southeastern Freight Lines, and WinShape could benefit your group or organization. Root Loud's focus is:

- Strategic planning
- Educational initiatives
  - Sales & customer service
  - People development
- Leadership
- Technology implementation

For churches and non-profits, Mitch focuses on the following areas:
- Life priorities
- Marriage and family balance
- Leadership in the home
- Removing the junk in your life

Go to www.mitchdsmith.com and www.rootloud.com to view our current curriculum, services, and event dates.